THE LAND OF
milk
&money

LESSONS LEARNED & BUSINESS EARNED
FROM WOMEN IN DAIRY

BY ABBE & MADELINE TURNER

WITH CONTRIBUTORS ESTELLE BROWN &
AMBER SATTELBERG

The Land of Milk & Money: Lessons Learned and Business Earned from Women in Dairy by Abbe and Madeline Turner with contributors Estelle Brown and Amber Sattleberg

Copyright: 2019 Abbe Turner
Cover & Inset Images: ©Shutterstock

Paperback ISBN: 978-0-578-57001-3

First published in May 2019 by
Airloom, LLC
2960 Essex Road   Wheeling, WV   304-810-2595
Cleveland Heights, OH 44118   Athens, OH   740-381-7509
www.theairloomcompany.com   Cleveland, OH   216-816-0308

Cover and Interior Design by Airloom
Printed in the United States of America

AIRLOOM is a dream company,
growing good ideas in Art, Business, and Community.

With roots in Appalachian Ohio + West Virginia,
Bearing the good fruit of human worth + hard work,
AIRLOOM invites you to share your good ideas by
email, letter, call or text.

To All the Goats I've Loved Before

FOREWORD

LESLIE SCHALLER, *ACEnet*

A cottage industry of dairy and livestock operators are meeting the growing demand for local food. As the farm-to-table movement gains traction throughout Ohio, new food and farm entrepreneurs are innovating in the dairy sector. Sleeves have been rolled up and rules have been adapted. Artisanal dairies and premier cheesemakers keep popping up in rural and urban places. When you dig deep into the turbulent times of the last few decades in dairy, innovation was the only choice. And to no one's surprise, it is the women who lead the way!

Currently, a diverse ecosystem of farm operations, value-added products and market strategies has emerged. This publication is a great guide to experience, firsthand, the challenges and opportunities described through the personal narratives of our rural innovators. You will note patterns of innovation shared by so many of the women in dairy profiled here. From diversification to tenacity to flexibility, many of these stories illustrate the new ways women farmers are working to create rural livelihoods for themselves and families. At the same time, they are reanimating local food economies in the places and with the people they cherish. Many of the chapters highlight the ways women have deepened their understanding of market opportunities, mastered herd management and designed product lines that compete on a national scale. Understanding the needs within the marketplace has helped many to forge better approaches to connect with customers committed to local food and economic transition. Ohio is creating a new roadmap that can be a foundation for building sustainable communities in which small farms can still prosper.

My organization, the Appalachian Center for Economic Networks (ACEnet,) continues to design shared processing facilities in Athens and Nelsonville. The ACEnet Food and Farm Enterprise Center now offers meat processing and vegetable packaging capabilities. As more artisanal dairy products are developed, we hope our facilities can continue to bring resources to our longstanding farm users, as well as with the new up-and-comers, beginning farmers and regional distributors meeting the demand for local, farm-fresh food. All across the state, our local food economies are steered by many hearts and hands building a nourishing network that enriches us all.

OHIO WOMEN IN DAIRY
FARMS & BUSINESSES FEATURED IN THIS BOOK

1 - Ayars Family Farm
2 - Blue Jacket Dairy
3 - Black Locust
4 - Canal Junction Farmstead Cheese
5 - Clover Road Creamery
6 - Ferrum Moraine Farm
7 - Hastings Dairy
8 - Hershey Montessori School
9 - Integration Acres
10 - Jedidiah Farm
11 - Lamp Post Cheese
12 - Lucky Penny Creamery

13 - Marchant Manor
14 - Old Forge Dairy
15 - Pierre's French Ice Cream Co.
16 - Velvet Ice Cream
A - ACEnet
R - Rural Action
(Full Contact List on Page 158)

INTRODUCTION

ABBE TURNER, *Lucky Penny Farm*

This is a photo of my new office. I much prefer it to my prior offices in air-conditioned cubicles in big buildings, my desk surrounded by photos of family, farm animals and old barns. It is in this environment with room to breathe and wide open spaces (yes, a Dixie Chicks reference) that I do my best work... outside in fresh air.

I will open this book with an admission: I am still trying to make this work, I am still paying startup debts from 10 years ago and I have almost gone under many times, but as I write this the lights are on, we are still making dairy products and we are planning for a successful farmers' market season. Am I getting a bit too real here? Well, this book is the one I wanted to read 15 years ago when I was beginning my journey in the dairy goat world, as a young mom and as a small business owner. It is a compilation of stories of challenge, success, unintended comedy, loss, joy, strength and much more shared by the community of Ohio women in dairy. It is a place where we can learn from and share with each other.

So often, women say to me, "I wish I could do what you do." Well, this book encourages you to say, "Yes, I can do it, too!" In these pages, we will see ourselves and opportunities through others' frustrations, challenges, and accomplishments as we collectively work to build a thriving industry that is empowering, resilient, diversified, family-centered and female.

It is with curiosity and humor that I find myself compiling this work as I still struggle with the imposter syndrome, 10 years into it. Regardless of how much time, commitment and cash I have dumped into this quest over the past decade, on many days, I feel I'm still pretending to make cheese, to milk goats, to run a sustainable agricultural business. "Fake it 'til you make it" is one of my favorite sayings (I am still faking goat yoga). Now I find myself here, hoping the tools in the stories that I share, as well as other women's stories in this book, bring you value just as they have enriched Lucky Penny Creamery over the past 10 years.

The path we have chosen as women in agriculture — as caretakers of our land, livestock, cheeses, and families — is a difficult journey, yet it is full of simple gifts sprinkled with moments of intense frustration and incredible excitement. In between these moments, I often find myself asking, "Why am I doing this?" Or I lie awake in bed at night thinking, "How am I going to pull this one off?" Yet, between these moments of doubt, there is a knowing and a quiet bliss for the life I have chosen. All things considered, I accept the ups and downs of this crazy life, including having the milk parlor hit by lightning, the creamery roof caving in, winning national awards, delivering cheese to rock stars, kids in tow and having Oprah Magazine calling. Through all of this, along with many women in these pages, we have navigated our family-first, business-first priorities through brain-numbing exhaustion while trying to grow our fledgling companies as well as our farms and children.

MY NEW OFFICE

In 2009, I threw away all of my pantyhose and heels and never looked back with any longing at the 40-hour workweek, much preferring my 90-hour weeks in my Carhartts and muck boots. Maybe this isn't something to crow about, but my current fashion comes from the farm store. T-shirts that say, Goats are like potato chips, you can't have just one! If this sounds like you, then you're not crazy or alone, and you might enjoy this book as a testament to the community of strong women in the Ohio dairy industry. This is a book about diving in, letting go and "pivoting" again and again. Come on in, the water is fine.

This is not a book on cheesemaking or a hard business book. The library is filled with them and we have included a select few on our reading lists. One must-have book that I highly recommend is The Farmstead Creamery Advisor: The Complete Guide to Building and Running a Small, Farm-Based Cheese Business by Gianaclis Caldwell, published by Chelsea Green. This book, released in 2010, is an excellent text to use as a road map. My only regret is that Gianaclis didn't write this book five years earlier and save me tens of thousands of dollars in the process of building Lucky Penny Creamery. I suggest you buy two copies: one to take notes in and use journal style, and the other to keep pristine for your bookshelf.

This book you hold in your hands is divided into thematic sections, each highlighting strong women and their personal farm and dairy stories. In the *Why?* section, we welcome you to the community of women in dairy food production. In the *Who?* chapter, we stress the importance of Slow Money as an alternative financing mechanism, and Sarah Taylor of Jedidiah Farm offers inspiration through her commitment to family and organic farming.

The *When?* chapter is eloquently shared by Kandice Marchant and describes how changes in life can lead to a new path in cheesemaking. In the *What?* chapter, Gwenn Volkert explains generating additional income streams from the farm through value-added products — soap, felt and breeding stock.

The *Where?* chapter displays women with grit and integrity. Bonnie Ayars, Brenda Hastings, and Michelle Gorman each live out their dreams, share their farms, and educate youth. The *How?* chapter encompasses the nuts and bolts of a farm-based business, from the business plan to the marketing strategy. In this chapter, Angel King of Blue Jacket Dairy tackles work-life balance and setting boundaries for business and family.

The *Help* and *Home* chapters celebrate community and the human element of a small business with essays shared by young farmers Rebecca Oravets and Madeline Turner. Together, their vibrant energies represent the future of specialty dairy as well as women growing agriculture in Ohio.

The *Appendix* closes the book and puts the meat on the bones: all the documents, diagrams and forms I was looking for when starting Lucky Penny Creamery. This, in conjunction with The Farmstead Creamery Advisor text, provide a solid road map for your success.

Your journey will be your own and you will make your own mistakes, but if you can learn from the voices in this book, maybe you'll experience fewer hard knocks and your costs can be minimized.

In these pages, we will consider the many aspects of starting your business: your personal inventory, sources of capital, infrastructure and equipment, branding, regulatory compliance, when to pivot, the triple bottom line, telling your story, and the importance of community. In addition, we will provide resources, vendor contacts and helpful tools on this entrepreneurial trip with milk. And yes, we will talk about money — real hard numbers pertaining to cost — and how it may affect your path to success.

Admission #2 - I am not good with money (there, I said it...) and this is where we discuss outsourcing and building your skilled team. I apologize in advance if anything in this work makes you uncomfortable, but if it does, I ask you to pay attention to why it may.

Why now? Well, this book is particularly important today, as dairy farms across the country struggle to survive and maintain their way of life. Ohio dairy farmers are calling it quits at an alarming rate as milk prices continue to drop and farm expenses continue to rise. From October 2017 to January 2019 Ohio lost 267 dairy farms, one every other day equalling an 11% loss in total dairy farms over 15 months. If a family farm is considering value-added products to help save the farm and a family's livelihood, then my hope is that this book will be a useful tool.

My qualifications for writing this book are producing thousands of pounds of cheese and unfortunately, many bonehead moves that cost me time and money. Through it all, I have tried to produce healthy, delicious dairy products while serving my community. I do believe that doing good is good business as we strive for the triple bottom line of people, planet and profits and an agriculture we can all live with.

Thank you for sharing in this beautiful mess. Let's begin.

OHIO DAIRY FACTS

OHIO IS HOME TO ABOUT 2,200 DAIRY FARMS
The average herd size is about 118 cows per farm

There are about 40,000 dairy farms in the United States.

OHIO RANKS 11TH IN MILK PRODUCTION

Ohio produces 5.59 billion pounds or 650 million gallons of milk annually

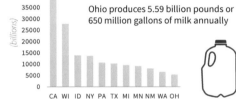

(billions)

CA WI ID NY PA TX MI MN NM WA OH

OHIO RANKS NATIONALLY

1st in Swiss cheese production

2nd in lowfat cottage cheese production

4th in total number of dairy manufacturing plants

5th in hard ice cream production

10th in all cheese production

11th in milk production

11th in number of dairy cows

There are about 261,000 dairy cows

 x10,000

There are 9.3 million dairy cows nationwide

97% of dairy farms nationwide are family-owned

97%

In fact, many farms have been in the family for mulitple generations.

Ohio dairy industry economic impact

The total economic impact of dairy products produced and sold in Ohio is **$23.44 billion**, which generates **114,053 jobs** for Ohioans.

Nationally, the dairy industry creates nearly 3 million U.S. jobs and has an overall economic impact of more than $628 billion.

American Dairy Association
MIDEAST

Drink-Milk.com

CONTENTS

WHY?

THE BIG PICTURE
WOMEN, FARMING, DAIRY, YOU

THE BIG PICTURE

Abbe Turner

We set out to make Lucky Penny Creamery a small-volume, high-quality boutique creamery. The company was designed to be an artisan alternative to industrialized, mass-produced dairy products that would accommodate chefs and foodies alike. We also hoped to please the little old ladies who came from other countries with cheeses that reminded them of their homeland. These are the highest compliments paid to a cheesemaker, to be told, "this tastes like my childhood." (Many had tears in their eyes as they spoke these words.) This is the reward for a challenging life dedicated to cheesemaking and dairy farming. Eating is a sacred act.

Our idealistic vision soon ran into the realities of big business and the challenges of being small in a big world, economies of scale, regulatory compliance, slotting fees, right-sized equipment, third-party audits, certifications and more. There was even a challenge to the definition of "local" or "natural." This was disheartening to me, as I wanted to be better, not bigger. I wanted to do something worthwhile to support my community, my local farmers and women in dairy. Are these my people? Is this my place? All signs pointed to "Yes" and I was called to be part of a movement to promote a healthy and just food system, reconnecting people with fertile soils and traditional grass-based dairy products for the pleasure of it all, as well as for the health of the planet.

Ever under-capitalized, every twist and turn led to somewhere new. For me, it led to a decade of dynamic, disruptive and dramatic experiences, from winning national awards to the dairy getting hit by lightning. In the end and through it all I led with my heart, determined to produce fresh, nutritious, affordable dairy products grown locally and with the care and well-being of the land, workers and animals a collective priority.

At the time, I didn't realize that I was working within the philosophies of Slow Food, a movement and organization that inspires individuals and communities to change the world through food that is good, clean and fair for all. Slow Food believes that culturally appropriate, nutritious food is a human right, clean soil and water should be protected for future generations, and labor should be dignified from field to fork. Healthy soil = Healthy food = Healthy people = Good, clean and fair.

LUCKY PENNY CHEVRE

And so began the journey to build soil, build social capital, build bridges among diverse peoples, build community wealth and build a thriving, sustainable food business. As Slow Food USA states, "We believe that everyone, every day, should be able to eat food that is good for them, good for producers and good for the planet." Amen.

WOMEN, FARMING, DAIRY, YOU

Madeline Turner

You belong here.

In this industry, today. Not only is there space for you, you have the right to be here. Anyone who wants to develop a relationship with the land should have the ability to do so; connecting with the land and methods of food production is a fundamental right. Farming, through the unique relationship one develops with the land through cultivation, accesses specific and meaningful aspects of identity, spirituality, and social movements.

We enter this industry knowing that there needs to be serious redefinition of what it means to be a farmer; being a farmer is far removed from being an old white man in boots and overalls. This false perception is just a single-sided perception of what it means to be a farmer and isn't representative of the people whose work allows the industry to stay afloat. Believing in a particular vision of what a farmer ought look like erases current realities of indigenous peoples and migrant laborers working the land in the United States and that women have been bringing something unique to the work of caring for the land for as long as humans have been practicing agriculture.

The dairy industry in the United States stands in a terrible light. Action, by a new generation of small food business leaders, is necessary in order for it to survive. Across the country, hundreds of dairy farms close every month. The dairy industry is proven to be one of the hardest to be in, and without sufficient capital, it is nearly impossible to succeed. Lucky Penny Creamery has been in business for ten years, but has barely made any profit. According to the American Cheese Society 2016 Annual report, approximately 2,000 of the United States' over 9,000 cheesemaking operations turned a profit, with approximately 5,000 of those businesses reporting profits under $500,000.

I do not write this to discourage you from entering, rather, this book exists to empower you to embrace all that the industry has to offer with full knowledge of the depth of the struggle and of how beautiful it is. No matter the intensity of the situation, however, there are pathways forward. As the new generation of farmers and food based entrepreneurs, you are uniquely situated to transform your communities. The industry is in

OLD FORGE AYRSHIRES

desperate need of a new voice to lead it on a path to a more sustainable future. No matter who you are, you have a right and responsibility to connect with the land. Not only is there space for you here, there is room and fertile soil within which you can grow.

WHO?

ABBE TURNER, LUCKY PENNY FARM

SLOW MONEY

SARAH TAYLOR, JEDIDIAH FARM

ABBE TURNER

Lucky Penny Farm

What to Do with all that Milk!

Abbe had fun introducing a herd of dairy goats to her century farm in northeast Ohio, but soon she had a problem on her hands: What to do with all that milk they produced! Soon, one thing led to the other and within a two-year span, Lucky Penny Creamery materialized.

First, Abbe learned how to make handcrafted cheese and confections… then how to perfect the process. A Slow Food Terra Madre Delegate, Turner represented the Cleveland Slow Food Convivium in Turin, Italy in 2008 — the same year her Cajeta (traditional Mexican caramel dessert sauce made from goat milk) earned second place in the American Dairy Goat Association's Amateur Confection Contest. In 2012, Abbe launched Lucky Penny Cajeta nationally at the Fancy Food Show in Washington, D.C.

These developments transformed Abbe from a home-based artisan into an innovative entrepreneur operating on a shoestring budget. Unable to afford a prime piece of real estate, she became a catalyst for economic revitalization in Kent through adaptive re-use of an old building. She converted an old Union Hall into a state-licensed dairy plant, establishing Lucky Penny Creamery and Lucky Penny Candy in 2010. The artisanal Chèvre, feta and ricotta produced there have helped Abbe meet high demand by regional chefs who prefer Lucky Penny products to bolster their own brands.

Ever the optimist, Abbe sees constraints and roadblocks simply as starting points. From there, she finds creative solutions by pivoting toward partnerships, grants, investors, community development or agricultural initiatives, Slow Money or crowdfunding platforms.

Abbe made a major pivot in the Spring of 2017 when it became time to improve and expand Lucky Penny Creamery operations. The creamery had operated for eight years in the old Labor Temple building, during which time Abbe earned a national reputation for turning out a wide range of fresh goat and cow cheeses. But sourcing the high-quality milk, transporting it to Kent, then making the cheeses herself had become utterly time consuming. She could not keep up with demand for product, let alone the demands of business and family life.

ABBE TURNER

Consequently, Abbe pivoted and partnered with Paint Valley Farms, a source of much of the goat and cow milk which Abbe had used over the years, transitioning LPC production to the Paint Valley Farm 40 miles from Kent, outside Beach City. Paint Valley Farm is an Amish business focusing on milk bottling and cheesemaking.

The new arrangement affords dedicated and dependable cheesemaking help, the efficiencies of not having to truck all the milk to Kent before using it, and shortening the time and distance from fresh milk to quality, consistent cheese.

Abbe's entrepreneurial agricultural lifestyle choice requires personal sacrifice, strength to push forward and flexibility to pivot as needed. Things don't always turn out as planned, and in order to have the best outcomes for family, community, and business, sometimes radical change is necessary although unexpected and not included in your business plan. Abbe says the rewards she reaps may not seem dramatic, but they are frequent and precious, like lucky pennies collected in a jar.

SLOW MONEY

Abbe Turner

Fueling the Economy, One Pound of Cheese at a Time

Lucky Penny Creamery would not have been possible without the alternative funding mechanism of Slow Money, investments from family, friends, and community when we were not able to secure traditional financing from any local banks or government agencies.

Slow Money is a national movement comprising people dedicated to helping food and farm entrepreneurs thrive by offering a formula for a new type of capitalism. They believe that in order to enhance food safety and food security, they promote cultural and ecological health and diversity, and accelerate the transition from an economy based on extraction and consumption to an economy based on preservation and restoration. Below are the beliefs of the Slow Money Principles:

1. We must bring money back down to earth.

2. There is such a thing as money that is too fast, companies that are too big, and finance that is too complex. Therefore, we must slow our money down — not all of it, of course, but enough to matter.

3. The 20th Century was the era of Buy Low/Sell High and Wealth Now/Philanthropy Later—what one venture capitalist called "the largest legal accumulation of wealth in history." The 21st Century will be the era of nurture capital, built around principles of carrying capacity, care of the commons, sense of place, diversity and nonviolence.

4. We must learn to invest as if food, farms and fertility matter. We must connect investors to the places where they live, creating healthy relationships and new sources of capital for small food enterprises.

5. Let us celebrate the new generation of entrepreneurs, consumers and investors who are showing the way from Making A Killing to Making a Living.

GOATS GRAZING AT
LUCKY PENNY FARM

6. Paul Newman said, "I just happen to think that in life we need to be a little like the farmer who puts back into the soil what he takes out." Recognizing the wisdom of these words, let us begin rebuilding our economy from the ground up, asking:
- What would the world be like if we invested 50% of our assets within 50 miles of where we live?
- What if there were a new generation of companies that gave away 50% of their profits?
- What if there were 50% more organic matter in our soil 50 years from now? *(www.slowmoneyalliance.org)*

The Slow Money journey began for Lucky Penny in 2008, when we began producing our candy from fresh goat milk from our farm, handcrafting the caramel according to a traditional recipe in open kettles. We seemed to be off to a great start for our fledgling artisan business, but timing is everything.

Unfortunately, 2008 was also the year the market crashed, and we could not obtain a penny of traditional loan-based funding. We went to nine banks and they all said, "No."

Persistence, flexibility and Slow Money eventually paid off. In 2010, Slow Money investors helped us to establish Lucky Penny Creamery in an old labor hall in Kent, Ohio, which specialized in fresh goat, sheep and cow cheeses and confections.

The renovation of this blighted facility was funded entirely by private investment from individuals, family and friends who support the Slow Money principles of bringing money back down to earth and investing as if food and farms matter. The Slow Money principles connect investors to the places where they live, creating vital relationships and new sources of capital for small food enterprises. By 2012 — thanks to a Slow Money grant from the Columbus, Ohio chapter — we launched Lucky Penny Candy at the National Association for the Specialty Food Trade (NASFT) Fancy Food Show.

Lucky Penny is entirely funded by 38 individuals who care about food and how it's produced. Slow Money investment often has a slower rate of return than conventional investments. People invest in Lucky Penny because they believe in our company's values, production methods, delicious products and our efforts to build a resilient agricultural economy, one pound of cheese at a time.

Our responsibility to our community for their support is demonstrated by paying it forward, working with more than a dozen farmers and by assisting the launches of new companies (i.e., Clover Road Creamery's fresh cream cheese from grass-fed cows). Lucky Penny is built on the belief that our value-added agricultural products, cheeses and candy from our dairy goats contribute to the health and happiness of our customers and the sustainability of our local food system.

Our Slow Money efforts have been recognized. We were honored to have earned the Kent Area Chamber of Commerce's IMMY Award, which recognizes local businesses that support economic retention, reinvestment and new facilities development. We chose to house Lucky Penny Creamery in a blighted building within city limits so we could participate in Kent's economic development as an urban farm processing operation. We wanted to build a thriving urban agricultural business, while inspiring others to believe in their dreams enough to move forward with them, hopefully using Slow Money investment as a tool for fuel. We would not be here today if not for Slow Money.

Lucky Penny Creamery is a rare link between farm and city, transforming a raw agricultural product into a premier chef's cheese in multiple urban markets: Cleveland, Columbus and Cincinnati. A healthy food system draws from local small farms which provide fresh, nutritionally superior food products for the consumer; not the over-processed, nutritionally depleted foods that are mass produced and transported cross-country to big box stores for maximum profit. Lucky Penny connects family farms to family tables, proving that a small business can make a big difference with the support of Slow Money.

This is a pivotal time for Lucky Penny. As we approach our 10th year of business — without one dime of bank loans to date — our next challenge is securing capital infrastructure investment so we can scale up production of our candy as well as increase the shelf life of our cheeses, both using new processing equipment instead of preservatives or chemical additives that would alter our clean and true flavors. It has taken time to get to this next stage but we have learned that good things come to those who wait.

Slow Money and Slow Food have reinforced our faith that we can strengthen our economy from the ground up, starting with food. Small business is the engine of the economy. We'd like to think it's fueled by cheese.

LUCKY PENNY
TOMME

SARAH TAYLOR

Jedidiah Farm & Studio | Westerville, OH

Born Off the Grid & Now Certified Organic

When I was born, I was delivered by my father in a 16-foot Airstream in Wickham State Park, Melbourne. My dad was a musician and my mother was a model. Vegan hippies through and through, we left the road to live on a piece of property off of a dirt road in rural upstate New York. There, using newly emerging principles of ecosystem mimicry for productive agriculture, my parents built a massive market garden and lived off the grid. We only ate what was in season and indigenous to our area: canning, drying or hunting what we needed over the winter seasons. From there, we moved to an Indian Reservation and later on, I helped my parents care for poultry and grow annual food crops on our small home in inner-city Memphis.

This background is relevant because as a new parent, it naturally made sense to me that the food we grow within our own ecosystem is more nutritious and tastes better. I knew that the food that my family and their friends raised nourished our bodies in a different way, and I recognized how it nourished the community around us. I already appreciated the inherent value of the labor and hard work that went into what we grew, and saw the reward as being worth the physical demands on my body. When our children came along, I wanted to give my children the same heritage, so we began to grow our own food.

When I had four kids, we lived in the high desert of New Mexico and lived on one-fifth of an acre where we grew hundreds of pounds of produce. We also raised laying hens, meat chickens and finally, dairy goats. Between the leaves of the garden, my children played in bare feet, and they learned to milk and feed the animals beside me. Over time, they learned how to contribute in a meaningful way, but there were lots of times along the way when they messed up what I was trying to accomplish, or they tried to help by pulling out my carrots or playing in manure. Along the way, I have observed that, when left to their natural instincts, children crave knowledge and learn quickly. Any person raising goats will tell you that if you try to force a kid to his mother's teat he will fight against you, but when you let nature take its course, a healthy kid will instinctively know to nurse because he craves nourishment. In the same way, children

SARAH TAYLOR

often fight against forced education but naturally crave information and search it out when empowered to do so. This holistic view of providing resources and information for learning has become my parenting mantra and it is what enables me to manage a farm while raising six children. With a partner who travels frequently for work, we are careful to not have any system on the farm that is too large or unwieldy for a woman or child to manage. Together, we work in community to create an environment that we love where people, plants and animals thrive together.

After four years of living on our current homestead in Ohio, I was ready to begin my journey of a woman-owned business. In August 2017, the month that my youngest child weaned, I filed my LLC and started Jedidiah Farm. The community has been incredibly supportive of our efforts and we currently have our certified organic chicken in three stores within the Columbus area. My children provide most of the daily care of our chickens, as well as assisting in every goat birth and raising the bottle for kids when necessary. They are fluent at milking and most are beginning to recognize the basics of nutrition and soil health that serve as building blocks for healthy pastured livestock. When people ask me how I do everything here on the farm the answer is easy: I don't. Our family is its own little ecosystem with each member contributing as they are able to the greater whole. Alone, I could only accomplish what one person can do, but together with my children, we can accomplish much. The narrative of my business has closely followed the narrative of our family and the ethics of our land management. We begin with healthy soil (instinct, potential, connection), we direct and cultivate but do not force our way (knowledge, opportunity, excellence) and we achieve quantifiable results (resilient humans, healthy community, excellent products) This is a narrative that my customers connect with, and it is the building block for my brand.

My journey in dairy goat production began about eight years ago in rural New Mexico when I was searching for reliable access to nutritious, local food for my family. We originally started out with a few goats from Craigslist but quickly swapped them out for higher-quality purebred Nubians from one of the country's top creameries: Black Mesa Ranch in Snowflake, Arizona. Prior to our investment in registered stock, my cheap Craigslist goats taught me a hard but valuable lesson: although the initial cost of an inexpensive goat makes them seem like a great bargain, the long-term costs almost always far outweigh any initial benefits. With those first goats, I got a crash course in nutrition management, health care, parasite control, disease detection and prevention, and lactation issues, which have proven to be invaluable as a herd manager down the road.

When we moved across the country for greener pastures in Ohio, I brought our initial brood does with us and have continued to add nationally recognized production and show genetics from across the country. We have shipped in bucklings from as far away as Washington state and we are committed to our values of healthy animals with strong lactations who thrive under a holistic management program. As a certified Organic farm, our animals need to grow and produce well without the use of chemical de-wormers, artificial supplements, commercial cocci prevention or high test Roundup-ready alfalfa. Often, we have to cull hard for the qualities we want and think outside the box — especially when it comes to sourcing feeds that fit within our holistic values.

As a small herd of no more than 12 brood does, each animal has to pull their weight in order to help us achieve our objectives. For this reason, we are members of the American Dairy Goat Association's "ADGA Plus" program, which gives us access to additional metrics for evaluating productivity and genetic worth. Through ADGA Plus, we can have professional evaluations done on the conformation of our animals, and monthly tests for milk components such as butterfat and protein. We also DNA test our animals to select for the Alpha S1 Casein, which has been associated with higher volume and a stronger curd when cheesemaking.

One of the most valuable resources I have created for my own benefit is a simple Excel document where I can input monthly milk weights from each doe to track lactation. This dynamic tool allows me not only to stagger freshening dates based on production needs throughout the season and to evaluate performance when I make changes to our management routine, but also to project with reasonable accuracy how much a first freshener can be expected to produce based on her genetic predisposition for performance curves. With this simple form, I can tell you how much milk we will likely have in August, and I can assess at a glance how much our production for this month has fluctuated relative to previous years.

Moving forward, we hope to continue selecting well for animals that thrive under the unique stressors that Ohio weather presents, and to equip others in our community with the tools for success in homestead dairy goat production. Last year, I began offering farm tours, private mentorship opportunities, and two focused classes on backyard dairy goat care, and we plan to build resources into our website with tools and tricks for success that will help others thrive down the road.

You can find information about our farm, family and goats at *www.jedidiahfarm.com.*

JEDIDIAH FARM

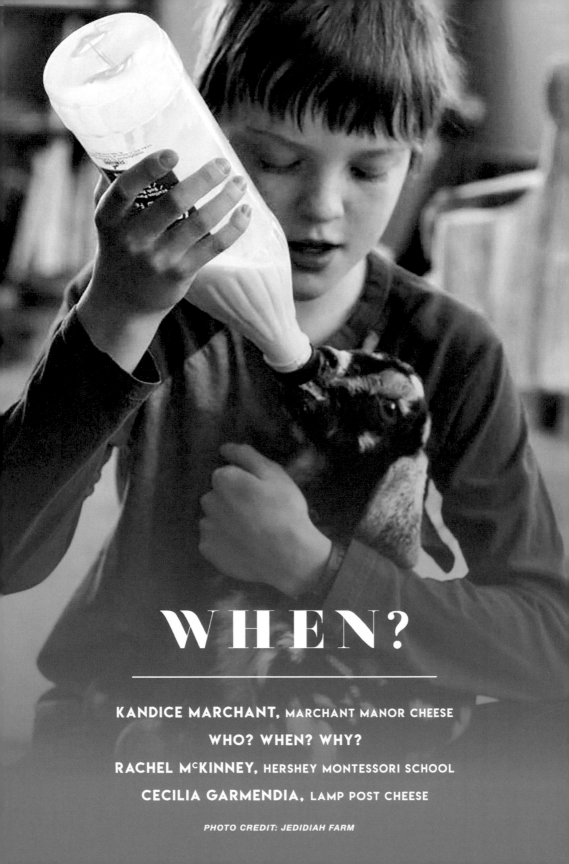

WHEN?

KANDICE MARCHANT, MARCHANT MANOR CHEESE
WHO? WHEN? WHY?
RACHEL MᶜKINNEY, HERSHEY MONTESSORI SCHOOL
CECILIA GARMENDIA, LAMP POST CHEESE

PHOTO CREDIT: JEDIDIAH FARM

KANDICE MARCHANT

Marchant Manor Cheese | Cleveland Heights, Ohio

Love, Loss & Cheese

Born in Wisconsin, I suppose I have always loved cheese. However, the cheese of my childhood was mostly non-memorable Colby, Pepper Jack and shrink-wrapped cheddar against a backdrop of cheese hats and large cow sculptures outside of cheese castles. It wasn't until I was in medical school at Case Western Reserve University (CWRU) in Cleveland, OH where I met and married a dashing Englishman, that my love of cheese was firmly solidified. Roger and I traveled in England and throughout Europe, where I was introduced to the tradition of a cheese course after dinner.

The sheer variety and nuances of farmstead and artisan cheeses amazed me and I became a devotee of the cheese course; who needs dessert when you can have luscious cheeses with the last of the meal's wine? I especially loved the small and soft cheeses — the oozier and smellier the better! There was one time in the south of France where a three-tiered "chariot du fromage" rolled up to the table after dinner and I was in heaven! So many cheeses, so little time!

My love of cheese remained in the background while I completed my medical degree in 1986, obtained a Ph.D. in polymer science, and had two wonderful daughters, Eleanor and Alexandra. Roger became a professor at CWRU, where he and I had a joint NIH research program. One of the benefits of a research career is that we traveled a lot, presenting research data, which gave us the opportunity to try local cheeses wherever we traveled. I was known to "smuggle" raw milk cheeses from France, Italy and England back home, making sure to wrap them in zip-lock bags to avoid smelling out the entire plane.

After my initial medical training, I became a pathologist at Cleveland Clinic and eventually became Medical Director of the blood coagulation laboratory. In 2006, I was appointed Chair of the Pathology and Laboratory Medicine Institute, the first woman at Cleveland Clinic to head a clinical institute. This was an incredibly busy job, where I oversaw about 1,500 people and was responsible for laboratory testing at eight hospitals and 15 family health centers, and helped build a new laboratory building. Needless to say, cheese wasn't at the top of my mind during this time!

KANDICE MARCHANT

However, as a break, Roger surprised me with a trip to Murray's in New York for a three-day cheese "boot camp" where I tasted about 75 cheeses, complete with wine, beer and food pairings. It was an eye-opening weekend, where I was introduced to milk and cheese chemistry. I remember an ah-ha moment that would probably only excite a pathologist, where I learned the chemistry of how milk is coagulated and transformed into curds and whey, not so very different from how blood coagulation occurs.

If my life had stayed the same, I doubt whether my cheese journey would have progressed much further than interested curiosity. But my life did change. In 2011, I was diagnosed with breast cancer and underwent multiple surgeries, chemotherapy and radiation therapy. This was a real shock which made me realize how quickly life can change and that you have to appreciate every day. I remember seeing a sign in the radiation oncology area that said, "Be grateful for the gift of today; that's why we call it the present."

Then, in 2013, just as I was pretty much back to normal, my husband was diagnosed with metastatic cancer. I was home with Roger as much as possible, despite continuing to work as the Institute Chair. During long days as Roger's caregiver, I started looking for activities that I could do at home. One fortuitous weekend, I attended a cheese benefit event at a local cooking school. There, I met Jean MacKenzie, who started making goat cheese and founded MacKenzie Creamery after leaving a career in real estate. Stimulated, I bought books on cheesemaking and determined to make cheese at home, which was something I could do while I cared for Roger. My first attempts were dismal failures. I tried making goat cheese but didn't realize that ultra-pasteurized milk will never coagulate to curds and whey. After waiting for curd formation for two days, I threw out the batch. My first attempt at feta cheese was so salty that Roger spat it out when he tasted it! My second batch of feta turned to mush in the brine.

Cheesemaking was put on hold as Roger's condition worsened through multiple surgeries and chemotherapy. When he passed away in early 2014, there was a huge hole at home and at work, as we had been best friends as well as research collaborators. Looking for activities to ease the loneliness, I returned to cheesemaking and diligently worked my way through recipes in Gianaclis Caldwell's *Artisan Cheesemaking,* from ricotta to mozzarella to Gouda and cheddar. I bought larger and larger stock pots as cheese "vats" and then bought a wine refrigerator, which, set to 50°F, became a perfect small home cheese "cave."

Ever the academic, I started looking for cheesemaking courses to help improve my cheesemaking skills. The first was a two-week artisan cheesemaking course in the summer of 2015 at Sterling College in Craftsbury Common, Vermont, taught by

French cheesemaker Ivan Larcher. We covered cow breeds, milk and cheese chemistry and then hands-on cheesemaking for soft cheeses. I developed a unique appreciation for the small changes in milk, cultures and aging techniques that make huge differences in the final cheese! I also learned about cheese aging in the cellars at Jasper Hill Farms. The six aging cellars at Jasper Hill Farms are incredible and inspirational. About the size of a football field, some have cheeses on wood shelves 30 feet high and others are redolent with the smell of ammonia from soft cheeses. Needless to say, I came home from this course besotted with enthusiasm for cheesemaking and eager to develop unique cheeses at home.

Given the knowledge I had gained at Sterling, combined with my love of the soft, bloomy and washed rind cheeses of Europe, my cheesemaking attention turned to making bloomy-rind cheeses. My first attempts were a camembert, then ash-coated cheeses, then triple cream and washed rind cheeses using local grocery store milk. My family and friends told me that they really liked my soft cheeses, but I thought they were just humoring me and my weird hobby. My daughters, now grown and living in California and England, started to request that I bring "mommy cheese" when I visited them, and their friends flocked to the cheese tastings. I started to dream about developing a cheesemaking business when I joined the Ohio Cheese Guild as an enthusiast and started to get encouragement to develop my cheeses further.

In late 2016, Ohio City Provisions opened on the west side of Cleveland. This was an all-Ohio food location with a butcher, charcuterie and cheesemonger. In early 2017, I brought some of my cheeses in for the owner, Trevor Clatterbuck, to taste. He and the staff loved my cheeses and introduced me to some unique all-Guernsey milk that they sold at the store. Guernsey milk has a higher fat content than many other milk varieties and also has a rich yellow color from endogenous beta carotene in the milk. I was intrigued by the Guernsey milk and decided to try the "scientific experiment" of making parallel batches of my bloomy rind and washed rind cheeses with grocery store milk versus Guernsey milk. The differences were astonishing – a comparative taste test at Ohio City Provisions resulted in Trevor encouraging me to develop the Guernsey milk cheeses into something that he could sell.

Dreaming about having a cheesemaking business is one thing, but developing one while you are still working full time as a doctor is another thing altogether. My work days were typically 12 hours long and weekends were the only time available for thinking about or making cheese. My weekend time was shared with visiting my daughters or my aging mother in Wisconsin. Plus, Ohio dairy regulations don't allow commercial cheesemaking at home unless you have a completely separate facility. Taken together, this meant that I was time- and facility-challenged.

Through Trevor, however, I was introduced to a possible solution to the facility issue. Paint Valley Farms in Beach City, Ohio is an Amish facility where Guernsey milk is pasteurized and bottled. They also had a licensed cheesemaking facility, which was not used full-time. While their facility was not ideal for making small-batch soft cheeses (it had a massive cheddar vat taking up most of the room), I was able to adapt my cheesemaking processes. After some discussion, in 2018 I reached a space rental agreement with Paint Valley Farms, which allowed me to make cheeses under their license one weekend each month. Further incorporation, legal, insurance and logistical hurdles were accomplished and I started making cheeses for commercial sale in July 2018.

The next step was developing a name and brand identity, which was to focus on triple cream European-style cheeses. I had thought of capitalizing on my scientific lab background and calling the business "Lab Rat Cheese" with scientist names for the cheeses, like "Einstein Ash" or "Pasteur Peppercorn" but was quickly told that "rats don't sell much food!" I finally settled on calling the business "Marchant Manor Cheese" as an homage to Roger's English heritage; this led to English names for my European-style cheeses like "Elmstead Ash," a triple-cream ash-coated bloomy rind cheese; Elmstead Avenue was the street Roger grew up on in Birmingham, England. There was also "Henley," which is a unique barrel-shaped velvet rind cheese using a special mould called *Geotrichum candidum*; the cheese is named after the town in England (Henley in Arden) to which Roger and I had planned to retire; I guess Henley cheese is my new retirement plan! Next was "Lapworth," a peppercorn camembert, named after my favorite English pub featuring roaring wood fires.

So my cheesemaking weekends started in July 2018 at Paint Valley Farms. Making soft bloomy-rind cheeses is a time-consuming process. The initial process from milk, to curds, to cheeses takes almost two days and nights of handwork, draining, flipping and salting. Since the Amish dairy is run by generator, there is no light or heat after the generator is turned off at 5pm. Consequently, cheeses were tended in the middle of the night by flashlight and headlamp!

My initial cheeses were offered for sale in late 2018 at Ohio City Provisions in Cleveland and were well-received by a locavore clientele. Shortly thereafter, I was asked by Kent Rand at Weiland's Market in Columbus to stock my cheeses. They sold out quickly and I've been told that he has a waiting list for them. Interest from restaurants followed, with chefs wanting to include my cheeses on their cheese boards. This was especially gratifying to me, given that the cheese board was my original "hook" into the world of cheeses.

I've continued to expand the amount of cheese I make during my one cheesemaking week-end per month. I have a cheese-loving friend who now helps me due to the increased volume. Dr. Mary Barkley, now learning cheesemaking, is the former department chair of chemistry at Case Western Reserve University. I guess the two of us are the "Cheese Doctors!"

What's next in my cheese journey? Making cheese in Stark County one weekend a month has been a great start, but it is challenging due to its distance from Cleveland and production limitations. I am currently planning a licensed cheesemaking facility in Cleveland. I would be excited to have an urban cheesemaking/retail facility where the cheesemaking space is visible and interactive for customers. Given the current interest in artisan and farm-to-table food, it would give customers an understanding of how artisan cheese is produced, building excite-ment for the product. Taking that concept a step further, I'd also like to offer cheesemaking and cheese education classes – and even cheese/wine/beer pairing events, like the one at Murray's that started me on my cheese journey years ago. Needless to say, this level of effort may require some changes in my day job!

It's hard to tell where this journey will take me, but my life has been enriched by the love of cheese and love for my husband and family. The losses I've endured, while difficult, have helped give me new purpose and have opened up exciting cheese opportunities that I would never have fathomed before.

WHO? WHEN? WHY?

Abbe Turner

Now it's time to talk about you. The good news is that today is the day you can start your business. Congratulations and welcome to the wonderful world of Women in Dairy!

Did that make your heart flutter? It did for me, and that early excitement gave me energy and drive (businesses are kinda like love!). But as you think about the possibility, I want you to consider who you are, why you are doing this and the timing of this adventure in your life. These early, honest conversations with yourself are critical to your long-term happiness and success. Trust me. I learned this one the hard way, by messing it up.

Consider why you are starting this business. Are you fulfilling a lifelong dream or passion? Are you a proficient home cheesemaker and do your friends love your recipes? This was how I fell into the rabbit hole, as people said they loved the cheeses and wanted to buy some, so maybe I should go into business? It seemed like a good idea at the time, in 2006. The world was different then. Following a dream or passion certainly can bring great satisfaction, but research needs to be done to see whether or not it can also bring a living wage.

Are you interested in building community assets, such as a shared-use facility? With the high start-up cost to build a creamery operation, shared assets make sense. Are you part of (or married into) a long-standing dairy family tradition that possesses resources otherwise not available? An existing milking herd, an existing underutilized building, a farm store or already existing agritourism activities? Is this a way to integrate family or transition to the next generation? Or is the time now for a new project due to changes in your personal life or family structure?

Even with consideration of all the physical and financial assets you may (or may not) have, you are the most important asset to the plan. You are the "Who" of this equation.

Do you like to take chances? Are you able to work long hours without sleep? Do you learn from your mistakes? Do you like being in control? Do you have the stomach to gamble on an idea even if you're not sure it's going to work? And how quickly do you bounce back from failure? You will fail from time to time. We all do. All these questions and many more need to be considered and your honest self-assessment is very important at this stage of the game. And I mean honest. If I would have recognized my limitations early on, and acted on the truth of the situation, addressing challenges early and head on, it would have saved me a lot of money, heartache and grief.

And now the "When:" Gianaclis states in The Farmstead Creamery Advisor, "Don't choose this profession at the wrong time in your life if you have too many other life responsibilities — such as caring for young children or elderly parents, diminishing mental and physical energy, or any other burden that will be a major distraction — enter the field with caution."

Here's the "Why:" What comes naturally to you? What are you really good at and where do you feel clunky or awkward? Many entrepreneurs, including myself, fall into the trap that we're doing what we're good at because it's easy and pushing off those things that we don't like because we're busy or we don't have time, or we'll get to that later. The reality is, you should get to that first and put the right people in the right places so you have the freedom and bandwidth to excel at what you really are good at.

Your personal inventory should include interests and activities that you like, certainly your strengths but more importantly, your weaknesses. This way, early on in your company's growth and development, you can put the right people in the right places: where you are not strong.

The most important benefit of building your team early on is that it will fast-track you to success and allow you the breathing room to be able to focus on family, time for yourself and things that are important to you. I strongly encourage you to begin with legal, accounting, and other professional services while you are conceiving creating your product line. Calling your county, state and federal agencies that will have jurisdiction over your activities is also something to do early and as needed. I have always found these organizations to be helpful, accommodating and supportive of our farming and dairy activities.

Start making a list. Do the research. Take the first step. Now.

RACHEL M^CKINNEY *WITH* ELLA

Hershey Montessori School | Huntsburg, Ohio

Dairy Goats, Adolescence & Education

Serving adolescents (12 to 18 years old), The Huntsburg Campus of Hershey Montessori School has a working farm, residential housing, program barns, bio-shelter and classroom buildings on 97 acres of predominantly wooded land. As students interact on the farm and in their local community, they understand how society is organized and learn division of labor. Compassion, diplomacy and collaboration skills are developed through experiencing human interdependence. Relationships with animals, plants and the planet are also emphasized, as the importance of sustainability is personally experienced.

Dairy Goats are part of that experience!

It is probably worth knowing that I have had dairy goats in my life, on and off, since I was about 12 years old. We had dairy cows on our family farm, but they were sometimes large and, well, bossy – especially to a preteen. Don't get me wrong, I do also enjoy cows very much, but I have always loved how goats expect you to be part of their herd. I also enjoy the more practical aspects that goats produce milk and meat in a compact size.

When I came to Hershey Montessori School as science teacher and farm manager in 2002, I did not have housing for my pregnant goat. Since the school is located on a farm that is used for education and real-work experiences for adolescents, they graciously allowed me to house the goats. Seventeen years later, the management of the goat herd is one of the important aspects of the farm. We also raise a beef cow, pigs, chickens, and board a few horses.

Each year, students can choose a project to learn about the ruminants on the farm (cows and goats). One of our students, Ella, has been involved with the animals on the farm for most of her time at Hershey. Once she entered high school, she actually created an adjunct position as the general animal medical manager.

RACHEL McKINNEY

"This helped me engage deeper into two things I am passionate about, animals and medicine," she says. "I feel like the goats on our campus are the one breed that always has a consistent timeline and process. Every year I have been able to see how different people's reactions are to the process and being a part of that process has been a significant part of my middle school and high school years."

Our students learn all about the biology of ruminants and have a hand in organizing the breeding season of the does with our buck. There is always great anticipation as kidding season arrives. Supplies are checked and rechecked. Does are constantly monitored for the smallest sign that they might be going into labor. As it happens, most of the kidding happens right when we walk away for that briefest of moments, but every now and again someone gets to witness the arrival of new life.

The goat kids are socialized by our students and spring is one of the best times on the farm. For years, we have been dreaming of having a small goat dairy and using some of our own milk. We went through several plans and designs for a dairy, and two years ago, we finally finished the first stages of our dairy. We have a licensed milking room and milk house and currently use some of our milk to make goat milk soap.

We are hoping to either sell our milk to a cheese processor or use it to make cheese in our own kitchen. We are working on the next steps of that process, which include finding better methods for cooling our milk and acquiring an approved pasteurizer. Until we can achieve those steps, we are happy to care for our herd, make some soap, and enjoy all the kids (students and goats) playing in the pastures.

LEFT TO RIGHT: MADELINE, RACHEL, TEGAN, SAMANTHA & ELLA

CECILIA GARMENDIA

Lamp Post Cheese | Lebanon, Ohio

I am Cecilia Garmendia, the owner and cheesemaker at Lamp Post Cheese, founded in 2016 in response to the growing interest in local, artisan products. We are an urban cheesemaker company (we don't have animals) located in downtown Lebanon and our goal is to provide the urban community with the end-to-end experience that surrounds cheese. Our mission is driven by five guiding principles: Local, Artisan, Experience, Modern and Social Responsibility.

We are Artisans. We work in small batches and are hands-on to ensure the best-end product possible. We are not interested in a cookie cutter process, and we appreciate the type of variability that adds the uniqueness and character of artisan products.

We support Local. We support our local community. We always source our dairy from small local farms and we buy other ingredients locally when possible. We work with other local makers to enrich the community and provide value to our customers.

We provide rich Experiences. Lamp Post Cheese is about more than making and distributing cheese. We strive to provide a rich, fun and rewarding experience. We organize classes to learn about cheese, and events where we pair cheese with other products (beer, coffee, tea, wine, etc.).

We present a Modern image. We apply modern branding designs and strategies to update a commonly outmoded perception of cheese and cheese crafting.

We always act with Social Responsibility. At Lamp Post Cheese, social responsibility is our way of life. Our employees, the environment, our community, these are as important to Lamp Post Cheese as cheesemaking and we actively work to support, protect and improve them.

I am a biologist by training with a Ph.D. in Cell Biology. I was a researcher for more than eight years, studying how cells respond to changes in their environment, using yeast as a model organism. I was basically doing movies using microscopes and making mathematical models based on the data I was collecting. I grew up in Spain, lived in France for a total of seven years and then six years in Seattle before I moved to Lebanon, OH.

Living in Seattle, I met my now-husband and co-owner of Lamp Post Cheese, Ryan Tasseff, another scientist. One day, I was complaining about the price of good cheese in the US and he dared me to learn and make my own cheese. So I did that. I found a cheesemaker in Washington State who had classes for the type of cheese I was interested in (aged sheep's milk cheeses) and I started making cheese at home (we lived in an apartment). And because I am a nerd, I started reading books and scientific papers about cheese and cheesemaking.

That was eight years ago. After my Seattle experience, I got a job as a researcher in France for two years. I didn't need to make cheese there. And then, Ryan got a job here in Ohio. By then, my passion for cheese was greater than my love for science. Ryan and I thought that this was a good place to start a business and we jumped in, headfirst. He still has his job that pays the bills and I am running Lamp Post Cheese full-time.

In November 2016, I started renting the facility from another cheesemaker in Cincinnati (My Artisano Foods). I was making cheese one day a week, only 25 gallons of milk and selling at farmers markets and a few restaurants. In less than six months, the demand was higher than what I was producing and that small production was not really economically sustainable. I was just able to pay all the bills. So, we went ahead to get our own facility and we calculated that we needed to produce 10 times more to be economically sustainable at some point (meaning making enough money to earn a salary and to pay employees).

It took longer than expected to find a building, finish the renovations and start making cheese. We finally started to make cheese in the new facility in January 2019. We have a small retail store and a bar where we serve cheese boards and wine/beer. We sell other cheeses than ours and we focus on Ohio/Indiana/Kentucky cheesemakers, although we have some other ones that we like.

I wanted to make sheep's milk cheeses but we don't have a farm (and I don't see myself running one) and there is no sheep dairy nearby. So we make raw cow's milk cheeses. Right now, we don't have any batch ready to sell until April 2019.

It was easy to get a loan for the amount of money that we thought we needed. But to be sincere, I wish I had more money. The quality of the renovations of the building is mediocre, the equipment was cheap and we struggled to have it up and running. I am glad that Ryan is an engineer by training and he has managed to solve most of our problems. I feel like I waste a lot of time because things don't work well.

CECILIA GARMENDIA

I am also worried about the dairy farm situation. First of all, we don't have any dairy farm in our county. The closest farmer with whom we worked for a year decided to quit last year. He helped us find someone else, but we know that they are also struggling. I am hoping that because we pay them a higher price for the milk than the co-op, it will help them. But the source change meant to switch from Jersey cows to Holstein cows and I have to learn again how the seasonal variabilities will affect the final product.

I was surprised about the demand for artisan cheese around here. I still don't know if we will be able to sell all the cheese that we produce but I am hopeful. We are located between Cincinnati and Dayton where there are a lot of restaurants interested in the farm-to-fork concept. It also looks like there is a growing amount of the population looking for artisanal and local products.

One other thing that I miscalculated is the amount of help I need. At this moment, there are four people working at Lamp Post Cheese, two full-time and two part-time. I would need at least two more people to help with everything. Right now, I feel like I am running behind all the time and I don't get to do everything I need to do.

But even with all the work and the struggles, I am enjoying it more than my previous job. I enjoy making a product that people like. I enjoy talking about cheese and cheese production. I am very passionate about food in general and about learning how our food is produced. And I hope that through the company, I can help small, local producers to be more visible to the community.

WHAT?

PHOTO CREDIT: FERRUM MORAINE FARM

SHEILA SCHLATTER

Canal Junction Farmstead Cheese, LLC | Defiance, OH

Transitioning a 7th-Generation Farm from Traditional to Sustainable

Canal Junction Farm is located in northwest Ohio near Defiance, in part of what was known as the Great Black Swamp. Here at Canal Junction, my husband Ralph is the fifth generation to have farmed this land. Our children and grandchildren are the sixth and seventh generation on the family farm.

Ralph and I began farming together in 1976 and have worked side by side for many years! We started out as a very conventional dairy and grain farm. In 1993, we started building fences, planting grasses and clovers, and then turned the animals out to graze, transitioning the farm to a grass-based model. This change helped to revitalize and save our family's farm.

I was blessed to have been raised on a dairy farm in Wayne County, Ohio. So the transition to farming at Canal Junction was a natural transtition for me. I helped with milking, making hay and planting crops right after we were married. Ralph and I worked more closely with the milking herd and I spent many hours milking with small children in tow.

When we switched to grass-based farming, we also started direct marketing our meat products. In the early 2000s, we started researching how to also direct market dairy and cheese products. Our son Brian was our initial cheesemaker and worked hard to get Canal Junction Cheese started. When he got an opportunity to work in Ireland for a year, Ralph and I took over the cheese operation in 2014.

Today we make five kinds of raw milk cheeses. Our Charloe cheese has received awards — both ACS and Good Food Awards — and we are especially grateful because of all the hard work that goes into making artisanal cheeses. While Ralph is the head cheesemaker, I work as the assistant, specifically as CFO for the farm and the cheese business. I also work with sales, as the Mom who keeps everyone's schedules, and makes sure the right product is out the door at the right time!

RALPH & SHEILA SCHLATTER

We feel that we have a unique set of challenges, given our geographic location in northwest Ohio; not the first part of the country to embrace grassfed and sustainable agriculture!

I would share with other women interested in the dairy business to be ready to give a lot of time away from your families… know that your schedules will likely be disrupted from time to time. Also, know that you will have a great sense of accomplishment when you can feel that you have a small part in being a dairy producer.

COWS ON GRASS AT CANAL JUNCTION

I WANT TO MAKE CHEESE!

Creamery Preliminary Assessment

| Assess Personal Stability | Physical Emotional Mental | Skill Set | Financial Situation |

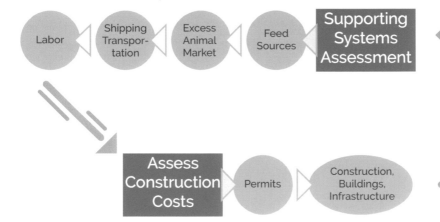

| Labor | Shipping Transportation | Excess Animal Market | Feed Sources | Supporting Systems Assessment |

| Assess Construction Costs | Permits | Construction, Buildings, Infrastructure |

Annie Warmke and Carie Starr
The Business of Goat Herding
Source: Gianaclis Caldwell,
www.gianacliscaldwell.com

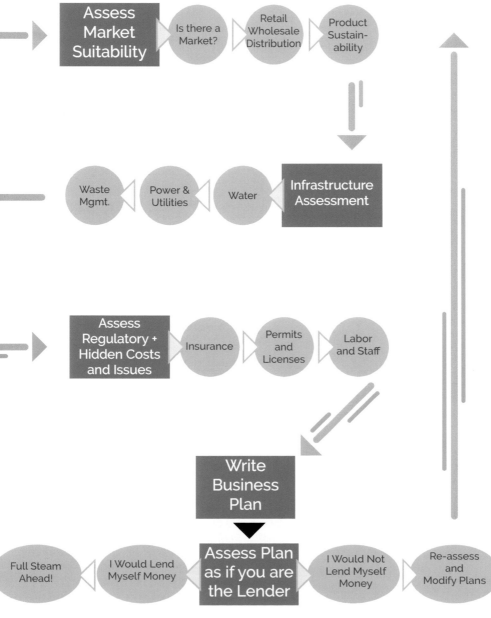

Assess Market Suitability → Is there a Market? → Retail Wholesale Distribution → Product Sustainability

Infrastructure Assessment → Water → Power & Utilities → Waste Mgmt.

Assess Regulatory + Hidden Costs and Issues → Insurance → Permits and Licenses → Labor and Staff

Write Business Plan

Assess Plan as if you are the Lender

Full Steam Ahead! ← I Would Lend Myself Money ← Assess Plan as if you are the Lender → I Would Not Lend Myself Money → Re-assess and Modify Plans

I WANT TO BE LICENSED!

Creamery Licensing Flow Chart

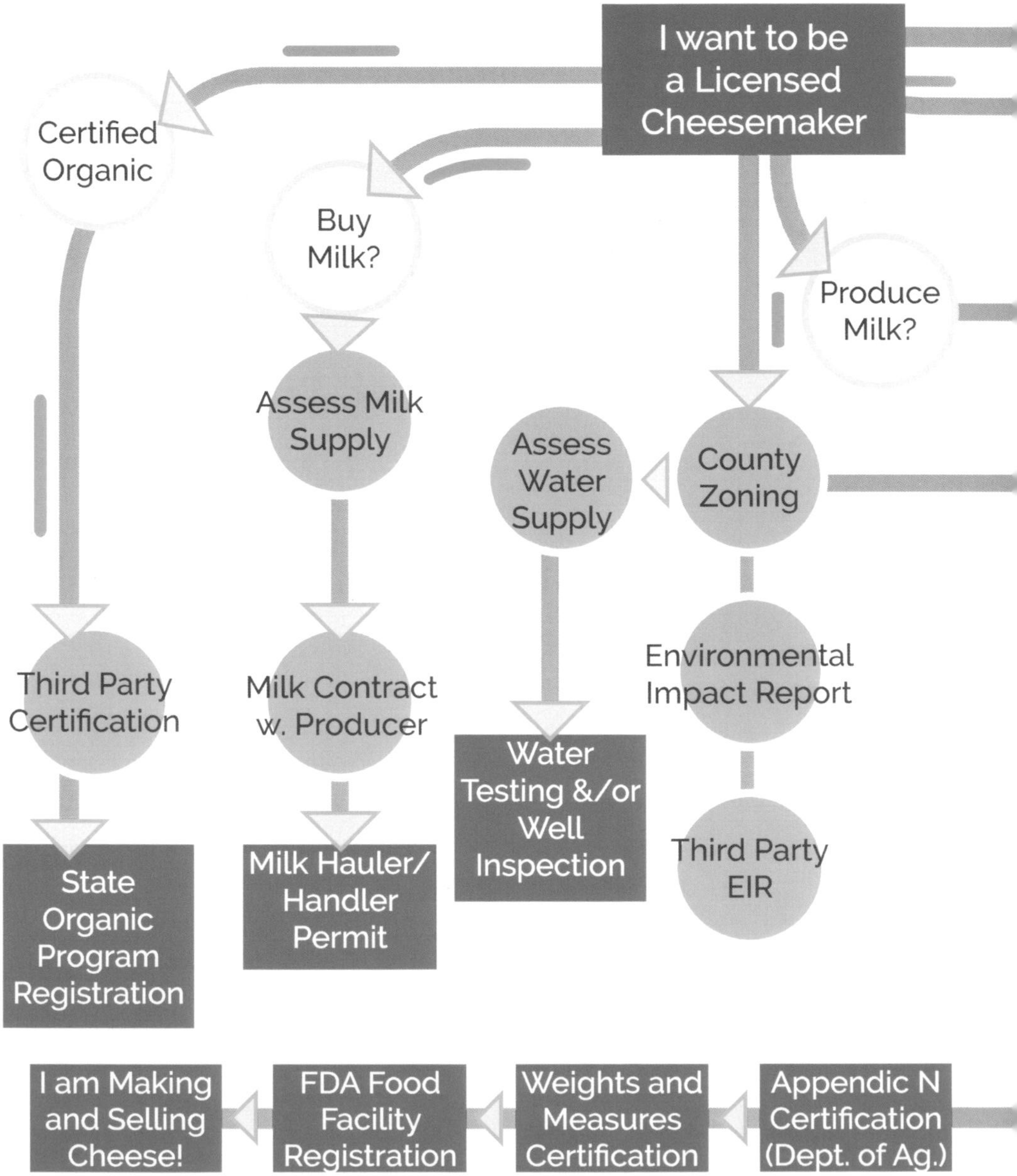

I want to be a Licensed Cheesemaker

Certified Organic

Buy Milk?

Produce Milk?

Assess Milk Supply

Assess Water Supply

County Zoning

Third Party Certification

Milk Contract w. Producer

Environmental Impact Report

State Organic Program Registration

Milk Hauler/ Handler Permit

Water Testing &/or Well Inspection

Third Party EIR

I am Making and Selling Cheese!

FDA Food Facility Registration

Weights and Measures Certification

Appendic N Certification (Dept. of Ag.)

Annie Warmke and Carie Starr
The Business of Goat Herding
Source: Gianaclis Caldwell,
www.gianacliscaldwell.com

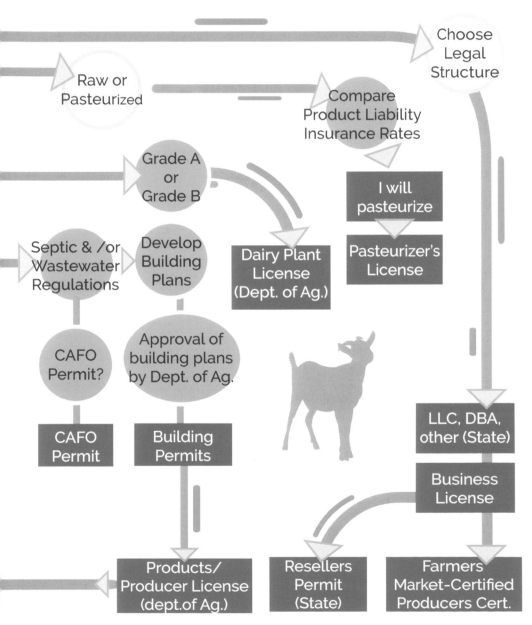

MILK, CHEESE, AND CHOICES — THE PRODUCT

Abbe Turner

By the time we had the farm and the goats for a few years, it became obvious that my lifestyle had to start paying for itself. Our goat herd was growing and the milk was flowing, so I began taking cheesemaking classes and learning to make cheese at home.

My first class was with Penn Soil RC&D in Mercer, Pennsylvania with Peter Dixon in the summer of 2006. The class was in a church basement kitchen and over the three days, we made many cheeses guided by Peter's knowledge, skill and unbelievable patience with our questions. I have taken many, many classes with Peter over the years and can't say enough about his courses. I learned more from his casual style and deep knowledge each time I took a class.

I love the science of milk and cheesemaking and was quickly hooked and ready to set the world on fire with my imaginary goat cheeses. When I arrived home, I called Parker Bosley, an ardent cheese lover, who suggested that I contact Ann Hauser, who made cheese for his restaurant. Soon after, I met with Ann, who was gracious and open and allowed me to buy creamery and farm equipment from her now-closed operation. When I asked her for advice about a woman going into the goat cheese business, her words were, "Run like hell!" This was not quite what I expected but I thought I was different, even special. To quote Carrie Underwood in her song *Champion*, "invincible, unbreakable, unstoppable, unshakeable," and so the journey began to make artisan goat cheese, handcrafted from the milk on Lucky Penny Farm.

In the summer of 2007, I took a beginner's cheesemaking class with Neville McNaughton at Clover Creek Cheese Cellar. This began the serious work of planning for a business making artisan cheeses. Neville helped us with technical consulting, plant layout and design, material specifications and early income projections. All of these numbers were overly optimistic, as we had no idea the economy was going to take a terrible turn for the worst, then crash and burn.

We began by planning to make fresh Chevre, Feta, Paneer and Halloumi in 2008. The numbers or Chevre were as follows:

- 50 Nubian goats milked (Protein 3.5% Fat 4.7%) and to selectively breed for protein to increase cheese yield
- 7 lbs per day milk produced per goat for 350 lbs per day of milk

- Chevre 16% yield
- 56 lbs of Chevre/day produced
- $1,120 retail value of cheese based upon $20 per lb
- $373.52 wholesale, based upon $6.67 per lb
- Solid guestimate was 300 days of milking: 50% retail sales/50% wholesale to distributor
- Total sales = $224,028

This is the optimism we built the business plan on and does not account for anything going wrong. But, oh boy, did it ever! Our timing couldn't have been worse to start a business. So it goes.

The Plan
(Sourced from *The Business of Farmstead Cheese, Yogurt and Bottled Milk Products* by Peter Dixon)

According to cheesemaking consultant Peter Dixon, you must consider certain things when starting a milk processing business. For our new business, we chose to:
- Be open to the public
- Use purchased milk
- Hire employees
- Be seasonal
- Use pasteurized milk
- Use Direct Vat Set Cultures
- Feed our whey to the pigs
- Direct retail and wholesale sales
- Urban creamery (versus at the farm)
- Delay the aging cave to phase 2

These choices had a number impacts, including:
- Type and size of equipment
- Type of packaging
- Labor needs
- Plant design
- Product cooler and cheese aging design
- Production scheduling
- Product pricing
- Food safety
- Septic system
- Distribution mechanism

These decisions determined the equipment and layout we needed, including:

- Raw milk room
- Pasteurization/production room
- Climate-controlled draining room (could be walk-in with Cool Bot)
- Mechanical room
- Finished product cooler
- Packing/shipping room
- Dry storage
- Delivery area
- Locker room/Laundry
- Restroom(s)
- Retail/visitor viewing room

The Farmstead Creamery Advisor by Gianaclis Caldwell is your Bible for this planning process. It is your complete guide to building and running a small, farm-based cheese business.

THE BIG DREAM - ON FARM PLAN NEVER BUILT

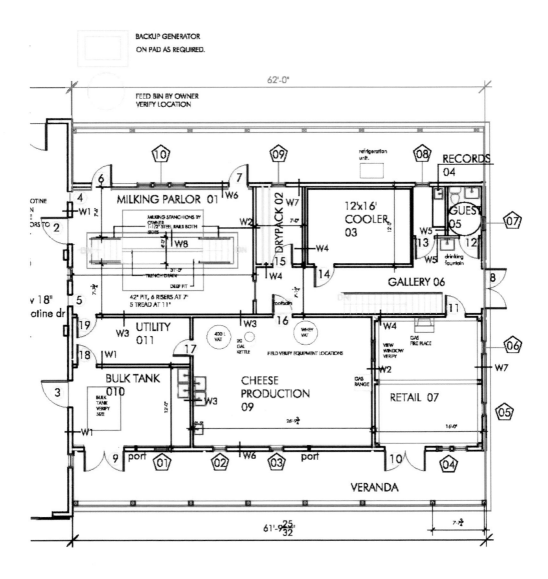

PROPOSED CREAMERY FLOOR PLAN

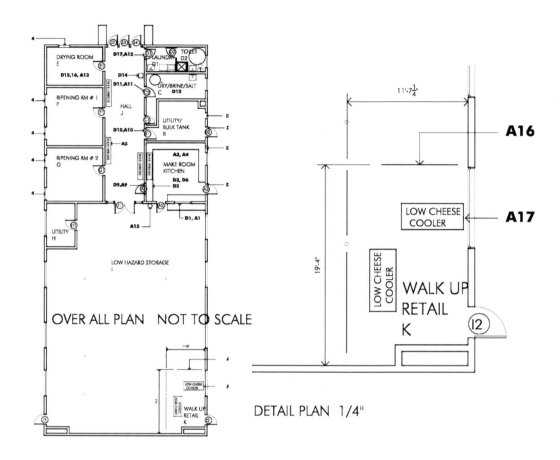

OVER ALL PLAN   NOT TO SCALE

DETAIL PLAN 1/4"

VALUE-ADDED PRODUCTS

Abbe Turner

Value-added products are a great way to drive more income back to our businesses and it can take many forms. In its own right, cheesemaking is changing the form of the commodity, raw milk, before it is marketed. But when considering value-added dairy products, they could also be kefir, yogurt, butter, ice cream or just a change in packaging for convenience-size or gift baskets. Many farms have had success with farm-to-table dinners, Airbnb farm stays, or even summer camps for inner-city kids.

Enhancing your company with a value-added product contributes to the economic sustainability of the farm and your community. Not only does it bring a higher percentage of the dollar back to you, the farmer, but it helps you build your brand, create new markets and extend your season. Value-added products are an engine for economic prosperity in rural and urban communities.

When considering a value-added product, it is important that it aligns with your company brand, is of high quality, is desirable to your customer and makes economical sense. It is helpful to do a mini business plan for each value-added enterprise to make sure everything adds to your bottom line. It also should be something that you're passionate about and that you love to do. I love working with goats, but I especially love to eat cheese!

As with any new venture, there are risks associated with value-added products, so you should check with your insurance agent to ensure you have the appropriate liability coverages for that specific product as well as where you may market it.

Many farmers markets now require vendors to hold a two million dollar liability coverage policy and for the individual

MARCHANT MANOR HENLEY

farmers markets to be named as otherwise insured parties on the policy. This is simple to do and your insurance agent will handle issuing the certificates.

One additional consideration of a value-added product is the increased handling of either the raw materials or the finished product, as each time a product is handled there may be more risks associated with it or different regulatory requirements for that specific product. Careful planning from the business perspective as well as from a food-safety perspective ensures that your new product will be safe, successful and welcomed by your loyal customers.

Although there is no sure-fire success formula for value-added products, a great place to start is with assistance from other farmers, entrepreneurs or food incubators that can help you determine the critical components for making a new product. That know-how, paired with sufficient capital to be able to launch a new enterprise, will get you farther down the road than going it alone. For instance, maybe there is an opportunity to share equipment or space on a truck for a delivery route. Any opportunity to work together to increase efficiencies and profitability should be strongly considered. In Ohio, we are very lucky to have ACEnet as a home for many new and thriving established food-based businesses. It is a valued and trusted resource for many new entrepreneurs.

At Lucky Penny, we started small with our value-added product ventures, beginning with goat milk soap as a way to build our brand and business knowledge prior to getting licensed to produce dairy products. It was a great business card — a bar of soap — to leave with clients. It was non-perishable, attractive, pertinent to the lifestyle of the customer and represented a piece of our farm. Next, we moved into producing goat milk fudge and selling that from Thanksgiving to Mother's Day, as it proved to be too difficult to keep the product intact during the heat of the farmers market season. Our goat milk candies won national awards and allowed us to take a perishable material, raw milk, and turn it into something with a six-month shelf life. This made sense to us as a way to manage excess milk flow, particularly during the flush of the season.

Sample Value-Added Text

Lucky Penny Farm features traditional goat dairy products crafted by hand using only the highest-quality local ingredients for our cheeses as well as our goat milk fudge. This is what distinguishes us. We raise our goats according to sustainable farm practices, we seed our own land to grow the hay that our goats eat, which provides us with the high-quality, nutrient-rich, creamy goat milk, and we manage the entire process from pasture to plate, bringing to market fresh, delicious goat love, from our family farm to your family table.

THE ACENET STORY

In 1985, a small group of community members committed to economic justice and building a healthy regional economy in Appalachia Ohio created The Appalachian Center for Economic Networks (ACEnet). Originally known as the Worker Owned Network, ACEnet focused on helping low-income people start worker-owned businesses. Their efforts gave rise to 10 worker cooperatives including Casa Nueva Restaurant & Cantina and Crumbs Bakery in the local food sector.

Since those early days, ACEnet has probably become best known as an anchor organization in Central Appalachia working with communities to rebuild local food infrastructure and catalyze food entrepreneurial ecosystems that put the needs of farmers, food processors, market partners and local customers first. Our approach connects buyers and sellers in local food value chains, where everyone wins. Communities invest in the promise of local foods and farms, as we measure the economic and social impacts of regional food economies.

By the early 1990s, ACEnet had established a small business incubator designed to give start-up businesses a head start by providing below-market rates for space and services such as reception, fax, computers and other resources. After opening the Cooperative Business Center on Columbus Road in Athens in 1991, the first mixed-use business incubator to serve low-income entrepreneurs, staff began researching a new model — kitchen incubator — which appealed to many farmers in southeast Ohio as a way to produce value-added products. At the outset, our Food Ventures Center was the first of this kind in Ohio to provide the licensed space, equipment and technical assistance to aspiring farm and food processors. Since 1995, The Food Ventures Center has served over 400 food producers, processors, farmers, retailers and distributors becoming one of the important linchpins in the Appalachia Ohio food economy. Over the past four years, ACEnet has built out additional processing, labeling, packaging, and warehousing capabilities in our Nelsonville Food and Farm Enterprise Center.

The ACEnet Food Ventures Center
ACEnet's Food Ventures Center provides a licensed commercial kitchen, thermal processing, flash freezing, packaging, food service and warehouse space to approximately 80 food processors, caterers, food trucks, distributors and farmers annually. Sector-focused training and technical assistance programs provide food and farm entrepreneurs

a diverse set of services: one to one business counseling, customized training programs, marketing workshops and webinars, food safety and industry-specific workforce training and the formation of support networks of community food practitioners.

The ACEnet Food and Farm Enterprise Center

ACEnet's Food & Farm Enterprise Center in Nelsonville, Ohio is licensed by the Ohio Department of Agriculture for ODA meat processing. Two new separate processing/packaging rooms for meat and produce were opened in 2018. The meat room allows clients to cut, grind, blast chill and vacuum package their meat in a low-temperature room, and also has equipment available to make sausage in the same area. Just outside the meat processing room, walk-in freezers are available for storage. Being able to operate in this licensed facility will allow producers and farmers to sell their products wholesale to retail stores or restaurants. The produce room provides producers and farmers with similar retail and wholesale opportunities. Many community partners are expanding processing for Farm to School markets.

Thirty-four years later, ACEnet continues to thrive as a regional organization. To learn more or view videos of our facilities visit *www.acenetworks.org* or follow us on Facebook, Instagram and our Youtube channel.

The Appalachian Center for Economic Networks (ACEnet) is a community-based economic development organization serving the 32 counties of Appalachia Ohio. ***The mission of ACEnet is to grow the regional economy by supporting entrepreneurs and strengthening economic sectors.*** *ACEnet staff accomplishes this mission by partnering with regional microenterprise and development practitioners to create a healthy local economy, allowing opportunity for all residents to start businesses, obtain quality jobs, and connect with other entrepreneurs for mutual benefit.*

GWENN VOLKERT

Ferrum Moraine Farm | Kent, OH

Small Animal Dairy Farming (We were really in it for the cheese!)

As I reflect over the past 10–12 years as a small animal dairy farmer, I am still amazed by all the ways our goats and sheep have enhanced our lives.

Our 16-acre Ferrum Moraine Farm is located just outside of Kent. We raise pure-bred registered Nubian dairy goats and purebred registered Icelandic sheep, which are a triple-purpose medium-sized sheep breed (milk, meat, wool). Of course, we have chickens too — doesn't everyone?

Our parents were not farmers but we both had opportunities to participate on farms in our youth — my husband helped a neighboring farm with bringing in hay during summers, and I spent time over several summers at my great aunt and uncle's family farm in Le Suer, Minnesota.

Our interest in starting a small dairy farm was ultimately driven by a desire to produce hand-crafted goat milk cheese like we had tasted during a trip to France. At the time, we lived in a small subdivision within the city limits of Kent — definitely not a place where we could have kept goats. It took several years of planning to get to the point where we could actually visualize our goat dairy dream becoming a reality. During those planning years, we started searching for farm property and reading just about anything we could find on raising dairy goats.

Then it seemed we were finally in a position to acquire our first goats. Actually, we were nowhere near ready — but one late spring afternoon, I discovered that my husband had no intention of building a barn until after we had purchased some goats. I was of the mind that the barn should be built first. While buying goats without having a barn may not sound like an ideal way to start, it actually worked out fine. We kept those first goats on our back porch for a few months while we figured out the barn issues.

As it turned out, the 20' by 10' barn was the perfect size for our first five goats and our first flock of chickens. Our starter goats and our small barn were quite inexpensive

JONATHAN & GWENN,
FERRUM MORAINE FARM

to build, and we were determined to not take on any debt to get our farm started. We purchased our first sheep the following year and it became clear we were going to need a bigger barn, as it turned out we were really enjoying our small farm and were anxious to make it bigger.

As would-be goat farmers, we failed to heed the common advice to purchase the highest quality stock we could afford. Don't get me wrong; I loved those first five goats so much and we learned more than I could have ever imagined over the first years of raising them. But we would be much further along in improving the quality of our herd if we had purchased higher quality stock (i.e., excellent milk genetics) to begin with. Nevertheless, there were numerous positive things about our small starter herd, especially with lower startup costs. A dairy goat from high performing parents can easily cost $1,200 or more per animal. Additionally, by not spending so much on starting stock, we had far less to lose if we had discovered that we really weren't cut out to be farmers.

Raising smaller dairy animals like goats and sheep was ideal for us, as they require much less land and infrastructure than their larger relatives. As mentioned earlier, we were really in it for the cheese. The suggested stocking rate for dairy goats is eight animals per acre. However, we have found that a somewhat lower stocking rate generally leads to fewer health problems and better land management, as rotating animals into different paddocks helps to break worm cycles and ensures the animals are getting the highest-quality forage. We currently pasture 12–16 does and five ewes on about six acres of pasture and 3–4 bucks and a ram or two in a separate two-acre pasture. Keeping ruminants in the northern latitudes requires putting up (or purchasing) a sizable amount of hay for use during the winter months. Raising our own hay is far less costly but did require a sizable investment in equipment. Luckily, used farm equipment is readily available, and as long as it's maintained, the equipment retains its value quite well.

The day-to-day work involved in keeping goats and sheep is not as much as you might think. On average, we spend 30 minutes each morning and evening doing farm chores; less in the winter when we are no longer milking and more during kidding season. While many dairy farmers depend on milk sales to keep the farm running, there are other ways to succeed. Our farm revenue streams from our goats have evolved over the years and are currently focused on production and sales of goats' milk soaps and lotions along with sales of quality breeding stock and freezer meat. As for our sheep, we sell lamb and wool as well as using some of the wool to create needle felted animals for sale.

When considering the financial benefits of raising small dairy animals, you shouldn't neglect how much money you will save as a result of having access to your own milk and meat. With your own milk supply, you can easily make cheese, butter, yogurt, and kefir for your family and have an ample supply of pasture-raised meat. While sales of breeding stock and freezer meat enabled us to keep up with yearly farm expenses and provided us with healthy inexpensive food, we were looking to find a way to have our farm make a little profit as well. The market for handmade health and beauty products has been steadily growing over the past decade. This ongoing trend is driven by people looking for local products made without synthetic ingredients.

It really is not difficult to make goats' milk soap and it doesn't take that much time, either. I have been making cold-process (CP) goats' milk soap with our own goats' milk for about four years now. After a year of tweaking recipes and trying out various color combinations and scent blends, I came up with several terrific recipes that I can produce for $1–$1.35 per bar in ingredient costs. Handmade soap can easily be sold for $5 or more per bar. With just a few goats, there is plenty of milk for making hundreds of bars of soap per month. If you make and sell 400 bars of soap each month, you can generate $2,000 per month or $24,000 per year. Ingredient costs would run approximately $400 per month, leaving you with $1,600 to cover your labor.

**FELTED WOOL FOX
HANDCRAFTED BY GWENN VOLKERT**

Soap is essentially what you get when you combine lye and fats. A number of oils can be used for the fat requirement. Goat milk itself is relatively high in fats, especially the milk for the Nubian goat breed — although the Nigerian dwarf breed's fat content is even higher, the yield per goat is significantly less. A number of websites and online videos are available to learn how to make at home a wide variety of cold-process goat milk soaps. If you are looking for a creative outlet as well as a way to use goats' milk, making soap is really worth trying.

Our sheep provide another avenue for income and a creative outlet, as their wool is great for the latest craze in fiber arts — needle felting. With just a few simple tools, one can create very life-like wool sculptures of just about anything. I have been focusing on farm animals and native wildlife (foxes, raccoons, coyotes, and various birds to name a few) but many other felters create beautiful wool "paintings" or use wool for wet-felting projects such as scarfs, bowls and vase-like vessels, rugs, and more. I have created many wet-felted vessels myself, along with drink coasters, placements, cat toys and more. Once again, the internet provides ample sources for learning how to needle felt and/or wet felt. Assuming one enjoys the process of creating wool sculptures, it's not too difficult to find people who will gladly pay you to make a memorial of a beloved pet. I have created memorial sculptures for most of the farm animals I have owned over the years and these sculptures help keep the memories of my past critters alive.

In closing, I hope I have succeeded in describing how small animal dairy farming can be a productive pursuit, even if you aren't able to sell your milk directly to the public or a processing plant. The benefits of keeping livestock go well beyond their financial aspects as well, especially when it comes to goats and sheep. All of my animals have very individual personalities and names which they respond to. The entire herd will eagerly follow us around the pasture much like pet dogs, and are always happy to have visitors stop by to offer scratches, treats or a friendly Maaaa or Baaa.

Goats and sheep can also provide a terrific opportunity to educate non-farm folks about the importance of supporting local farms and local conservation efforts in addition to providing a great place to visit just to be entertained by these delightful critters. I have yet to meet anyone who can hold back a smile when watching a couple of goats playing. And for me, that's worth just as much, if not more, than the profits we earn from raising them.

FERRUM MORAINE
GOAT MILK SOAP

WHAT'S THE MATTER WITH MANCHEGO?

Amber Sattelberg

Struggles in the U.S. Sheep Milk Market

Which came first: the cow's milk or the sheep's? The answer might surprise you.

Although sheep and cows have both been milked since around 500 AD, it wasn't until 1400 AD that cow's milk surpassed sheep's in popularity. That's right — the humble sheep was the original dairy cash cow. Nowadays, sheep milk production sits between camel milk and buffalo milk in its proportional contribution to the total tons of milk produced globally. While that is far below the quantity supplied by their bovine cousins, the unique properties of sheep milk make it an important contributor to the world dairy industry.

Higher in butterfat and protein than goat or cow milk, sheep milk lends itself to the production of cheese which has given us such delicacies as Feta, Manchego, Ricotta, Pecorino, Romano, Halloumi, and Roquefort, among others. In addition, the unique molecular composition of sheep milk allows it to be frozen and stored without affecting its usefulness for cheese production. The same cannot be said for cow or goat milk.

Composition of different kinds of milk

Species	% Solid	% Fat	% Protein	Calcium (mg)	Calories (kcal)
Human	12.5	4.38	1.03	32	70
Cow	12.01	3.34	3.29	119	69
Goat	12.97	4.14	3.56	134	69
Sheep	19.30	7.0	5.98	193	108

Source: The nutritional value of sheep milk by George F. W. Haenlein

LUCKY PENNY SHEEP MILK FETA

This might beg the question, why isn't sheep milk used more commonly (and why it is a relative novelty in the States)? The simple answer is that cows produce a much higher volume of milk per animal. The East Friesian, "The Holstein of the Sheep World," will produce, at most, 1,000 pounds of milk annually while the Holstein cow, "The Holstein of the Cow World," will produce 22,600 pounds of milk annually. Due to this vast disparity, it is no small wonder that sheep have settled lower in the dairy industry's totem pole. And yet, the United States imports about 66 million pounds of sheep milk annually, which indicates that there still exists a demand for this unique dairy product.

The 2010 Ohio Sheep Milk and Cheese Initiative sought to determine whether producers in Ohio might be able to use this market to their advantage and conducted a feasibility study regarding the same. This resulted in the start-up of several sheep dairying operations in the state among farmers, which ultimately have proven to be challenging in terms of profitability. Over the past few years, many of the farms that took advantage of the importation of East Friesian ewes have had to curtail their production or sell off their animals completely. Although there has been some speculation that the Ohio Sheep Milk and Cheese Initiative's less-than-desirable result stemmed from an imbalance between the effort put into generating supply vs. demand (the project was aimed at the producer's end and did not focus on generating marketing that would foster demand among the public), the OSMCI's struggles are not unique to the project.

In fact, the battle to keep sheep milk producers — well, productive — mirrors a national trend which was identified in the New York Times article, "Sheep's Milk Cheeses in U.S. Earn Ribbons but Little Profit." The piece identifies several sheep milk producers who have dedicated time and money to producing outstanding artisanal sheep cheeses which are recognized at fairs and in contests for their excellence, but which do not pull in the profit one might expect of award-winning cheeses. Through interviews with several producers, the author of the article concludes that the small volume of milk produced by ewes, as well as the short annual milking period (about 204 days), have contributed to the low viability of sheep dairying as a profitable financial venture for small producers. Being that the sheep dairy industry in Europe is much more well-developed, the price and volume of imported milk is much more attractive to cheesemakers in the United States compared to its domestically produced counterpart.

Despite the difficulties that small sheep dairies in the U.S. face, there are nevertheless farms that are managing to make their businesses profitable, so all hope is not lost. Whether by using hormone manipulation to ensure that there will be ewes to milk year 'round, diversifying dairy production through the fabrication of yogurt as well as cheese, and capturing a wider market through online sales of specialty sheep dairy products, producers are giving their best effort to help grow the sheep dairy industry in the U.S.

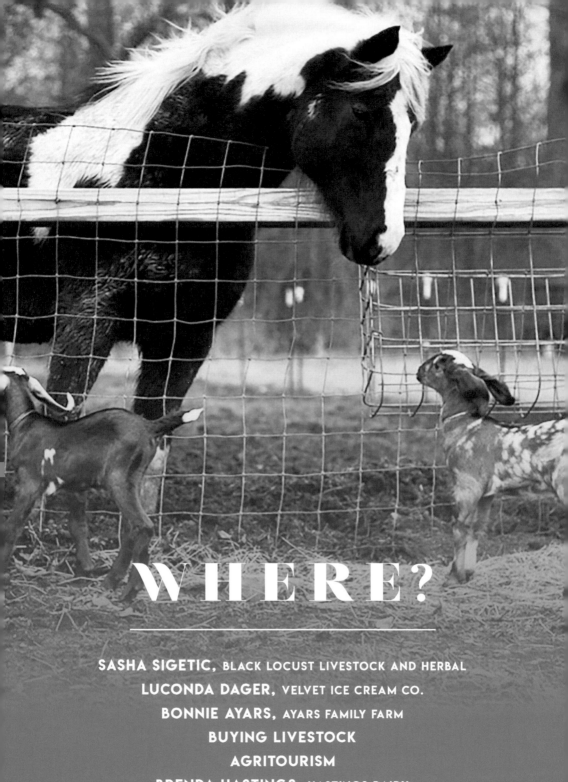

WHERE?

SASHA SIGETIC, BLACK LOCUST LIVESTOCK AND HERBAL

LUCONDA DAGER, VELVET ICE CREAM CO.

BONNIE AYARS, AYARS FAMILY FARM

BUYING LIVESTOCK

AGRITOURISM

BRENDA HASTINGS, HASTINGS DAIRY

MICHELLE GORMAN, INTEGRATION ACRES

PHOTO CREDIT: JEDIDIAH FARM

SASHA SIGETIC

Black Locust Livestock & Herbal | Albany, OH

Homesteading, Permaculture & Dairy Goats

Black Locust Livestock & Herbal is a small-scale goat dairy operated according to permaculture principles. This ethic offers no-waste, whole-system solutions that benefit both the humans and the animals on the farm, as well as the entire farm ecosystem. It's also a labor of love for owner and farmer Sasha Sigetic.

Sasha describes this mutually beneficial, closed-loop system as one in which she and her family rely on their herd of British Guernsey goats for their milk and meat. As a complement to the goats' diet of organic/GMO-free grain/alfalfa mix and grass/legume hay, Sasha runs them loose to forage in areas where invasive plants have overrun the farm, a process by which they not only gain nutrients but help to reclaim land previously abandoned by loggers and strip miners.

As of February 2019, Sasha's heritage breed herd consisted of eight females, two bucks, nine babies and a few more on the way. Sasha's plan is to maintain her breeding-up program into the 15th or 16th generation, at which point she will have achieved a pure BG breed.

Sasha finds the three-quarter size dairy goats ideal for producing nutrient-dense, flavorful milk and meat, delivering a high forage-to-milk conversion with little need for grain. She finds the British Guernseys a hearty breed, resistant to disease and death — "the perfect homesteading breed."

Homesteading is at the heart of Sasha's lifestyle. Having been raised in southeast Ohio, she left home to attend art school in Austin, Texas. While there, she deepened her commitment to nutrition and natural health, taking courses in permaculture certification. This experience introduced Sasha to goats and the dream was borne to raise her own herd some day.

After pursuing studies in ceramic and fiber arts in college, Sasha returned home to help care for her grandparents. In order to build her farm skills, she started working for Integration Acres, first milking goats for their creamery business, then becoming farm manager.

Along the way, Sasha bought a 106-acre parcel to reclaim and develop. She also started raising her own goats there. She and Ross Martin, along with their daughter, Mirna, have held the property for six years but just started living on it two-and-a-half years ago as homesteaders. Ross' woodworking skills have been put to good use on the homestead, both as main builder and breadwinner for the past nine years. But generating enough cash flow is a constant challenge.

Diversification is key to making both Sasha and her farm more profitable and self-sustaining. As for herself, Sasha is quite diversified. She works the farm; manages, milks and breeds her herd; operates a raw milk herd share; makes herbal tinctures, face creams and salves from plants foraged from their own land; teaches courses in sustainable resource management, pest management and husbandry at Hocking College; teaches ceramics and fiber arts at the Dairy Barn; and home-schools her 9-year-old daughter.

Sasha claims she's not too tired to maintain this frenetic pace for a while, "but I know I'll be tired when I'm 70 or 80, so I need to get busy diversifying this farm while I'm still young and physically able."

So in addition to her herd share program, Sasha and her family have also taken on landmates who are experts in food foresting and silvopasture. They are applying their

SASHA SIGETIC

sustainable food production/land management principles to nearly 70 acres of the farm. Once Mirna is ready to commit to more responsibilities on the homestead, Sasha is also planning for them to start raising chickens (egg layers and broilers), as well.

One challenge Sasha faced 10 years ago when she first entered the southeast Ohio farm scene as a young woman was gaining respect and credibility from the local agricultural community of mostly older men. But day after day and year after year, she did the work, gained mastery in managing goats, and eventually won over many a skeptic.

"Some of my neighbors have become my farm grandmas and grandpas," Sasha shares. "They go out of their way to let me know that I have managed to impress them with my work ethic. They also are happy to see someone younger taking up the mantle and carrying forward the family farm lifestyle. Now they even see me as an authority and stop to ask my advice. They're like, 'I know you... You're the Goat Lady!'"

No doubt, the life of a homesteader defies every notion of convenience. But for Sasha, that's part of the appeal. Convenience means eating processed foods, wasting precious resources and living in a self-serving and shortsighted manner. She is dedicated to the richer life, blessed by the rewards of hard work that benefits the land, the animals, the humans and the future.

"This is a hard way to make a living," she freely admits. "But this is a passion I'm not willing to give up. It's important to carry this way of life forward for the next generation. My daughter is already dreaming about the home she wants to build here when she grows up. She loves this life as much as I do, and she doesn't want to leave it behind for a life in the suburbs or the city."

LUCONDA DAGER

Velvet Ice Cream Company | Utica, OH

Leading a Fourth-Generation Ice Cream Company into the Future

Luconda Dager is the president of the Velvet Ice Cream Company, which was established in 1914. She represents the fourth generation of her family to lead the Utica, Ohio-based ice cream manufacturer. Luconda oversees all aspects of the 105-year-old company, which currently has 125 employees and produces and distributes more than five million gallons of ice cream every year.

Luconda took over the reins as president of Velvet Ice Cream in 2009. She also serves on the Board of Directors of International Dairy Foods Association; Midwest Dairy Foods Association; and The Woodward Local Food Initiative. Additionally, she is a trustee for Hervey Memorial Library in Utica. A frequent speaker and author in the dairy industry and on small and family business issues, Luconda is also active in the Conway Center for Family Business. In 2007, she was named to the Columbus Business First "Forty Under Forty" list for influential business leaders.

Luconda attended St. Francis de Sales School and graduated from Newark Catholic High School in Newark, Ohio. She studied business at the University of St. Frances in Ft. Wayne, Indiana and earned a bachelor's degree in 1991 from Xavier University in Cincinnati. She and her husband, Bill, live in Mt. Vernon with their daughter, Lauren.

Velvet Ice Cream was originally created by Joseph Dager, a first-generation Dager in America. He got started in the basement of a Utica confectionary in 1914 with three basic flavors: chocolate, vanilla, and strawberry. He also produced the ice needed to get the ice cream to various locations.

Today, Velvet Ice Cream products now include premium ice cream, sherbet, all-natural ice cream, yogurt and novelties such as ice cream sandwiches, push-ups and individual cups. The company has been located at Ye Olde Mill on Route 13 in Utica ever since the business was relocated there in 1960. Renovations have transformed the mill into a turn-of-the-century ice cream parlor, welcoming more than 150,000 people every year.

SIX **NEW** FLAVORS, SAME **GREAT** TASTE.

VELVET ICE CREAM

Distribution has also grown, with Velvet branches opening in Chillicothe, Cleveland, Cincinnati, Bucyrus, Ft. Wayne, Indianapolis, and Louisville throughout the years. In 2019, Velvet will be expanding into new markets such as Michigan and West Virginia, taking the 105-year-old ice cream company boldly into the future.

BONNIE AYARS

Madeline Turner

The Cowgirl in Residence at the Ohio State University

Bonnie Ayar's excited voice is unforgettable — sitting in her office in The Ohio State University's Animal Science Building where she works as a professor and in outreach, I learned precisely what it means to be a cowgirl. This is not a title I would issue lightly, though "Cowgirl" decorated the walls of Bonnie's office alongside ribbons and pictures of the Dairy Quizbowl teams she has coached, Bonnie exemplifies what it means to be a modern dairy cowgirl through her inexhaustible compassion and genuine grit. In killer combination, these two elements drive the dairy industry; without them, success is impossible.

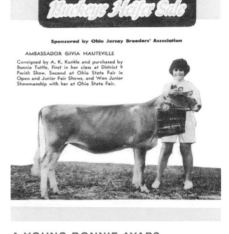

As Bonnie tells us her story, she peppers in dairy references as if they were universal truth. "I came to college on a cow," she says with a smile. Knee deep in Ohio dairy country, Bonnie Ayars grew up on a small dairy farm and participated in 4-H for the entirety of her teenage years. In order to finance her college education, her father told her to sell her prized cow and 4-H project — she was the first person in her family to graduate college, and told us that selling cows was the go-to when the family needed to pay for something. As a young woman in the mid-twentieth century, Bonnie always felt that she had to "earn it," as she wasn't allowed to judge or compete in ways she wanted to because she was a woman. This didn't stop her from pursuing her passion for the skill of judging cows, however, as she has been committed to educating youth over the last 46 years of her career.

A YOUNG BONNIE AYARS

She calls the farming and dairy world "agri-culture," with emphasis on the "culture." Nothing about farming is just a business — there are networks of communities and lifestyles attached to it. You are never just a dairy farmer because your day doesn't end

BONNIE AYARS

at 5:00 when you get off work; your life and your identity become tied to the joy and the trials of the work itself. Dairy is a distinct part of that culture — Bonnie, in her enthusiasm, demonstrates the grittiness and resilience necessary to be a woman in dairy.

Her current farm life follows the same flavor of her upbringing — just like raising animals or children, the journey has been spotted with trials and moments of joy. Milking 120 head of cow, the Ayars Family Farm has a revolving door and supports a variety of community and entrepreneurial endeavors, from educational farm tours to the 2017 Farm Aid concert. Dairy farming is a family affair — all of her children, though they have grown up, are all still involved; she tells us the farm stays strong because they are family to each other, and to the people who milk the cows or work in the barns. Despite working full time in Columbus, Bonnie still feeds the cows every day and still does all the farm's paperwork, telling us, with a smile, "I can do it all already so it doesn't make sense to have anyone else do it!" But all isn't smooth sailing — "just being creative will get you through a lot," she says, and it solidifies for me the sheer importance of staying positive, resilient, and creative in the face of the harshest adversity. Several years ago, the Ayars' lost their oldest son in a farm acccident. In her true and honest style, and as if in words of advice to any person looking to enter the industry, Ayars re-emphasizes the need to stay strong. "We do it because we are gritty. The real people that get through are the ones that push through," and "it's not for everyone, sometimes you just have to survive."

All of this proves that in order to thrive in dairy, you have to be as genuinely compassionate as you are hardworking. Community is key, and resilience takes many forms. Bonnie's life exemplifies the need for intergenerational community building — as someone who has routinely engaged and empowered youth, she sets the example for engaging with the future. Starting programs to incentivize participation Dairy 4-H and coaching Dairy Quizbowl are just some examples of the broad-reaching and impactful work she has done, telling us that she has seen multiple marriages among her students. With an understanding that learning happens both ways, Bonnie advocates for an attention to tradition but a willingness to innovate, to be "traditional in a different way" through connection to community. "New kids have to correct what we didn't do right, but I smile, because in the passing down of people, there's this transformation," she explains, and is right. Dairy is in constant dialogue between new and old, future and past, and it's not always easy: "This is life, it smells sometimes." She tells me there is room for diversity in dairy, and that there are spaces for women to work together. "Women doing these projects invest in each other," she reminds me, "bring your attitude, bring it on."

Bonnie Ayars personifies grit. Grit is more than just an identifier; it's a way of being, as Bonnie's story proves that the backbone of the country's dairy industry consists of people who are capable of being knocked down repeatedly by the hardest blows, but then able to get right back up again with a smile and a story to share. "Do your homework, get lots of experience, because this is not a job you can just walk away from," she advises, and when we ask about how to face adversity, she tells us "I invite anyone... if you have a problem or need to address something... to take your best shot at me, but I'll move on."

"Pave the way," she says. And we will; we must persevere with grit, love, and honesty.

WHERE TO GET YOUR LIVESTOCK

Amber Sattelberg

Breaking Down Your Decision

The first step in purchasing the animals that will drive your dairy production business is to define the aim of your operation. Will you be selling milk for consumption as-is, or will it be processed? Is volume or milk solid percentage more important to you? Are you interested in dealing with heritage breeds? Is there marketing value in electing a certain breed over another? These questions merit careful consideration before any money is spent on live animals and it will direct the manner in which you carry out the hunt for your ideal animals.

Once the aim of your operation has been well defined, it is time to consider the breed of livestock that best suits your needs. Take in to account the climate you live in as well as the production capabilities and temperaments of the breeds you're researching.

Armed with a list of breeds that will suit your needs, it's time to decide where to acquire your animals. The three avenues by which the great majority of animals will exchange hands are via auction, breeder or private party. The chart below is an abbreviated breakdown of pros and cons of each method of purchase.

JEDIDIAH FARM

Ultimately, it will be up to each producer to decide what they're looking for in their animals and their farm at large. While the above can serve as general guidelines for livestock purchasing, each producer (and each animal!) is different. Take a look around your area and online to get an idea of what is available to you, weigh your options and, most important of all, make sure you make a thorough examination of an animal, regardless of where you are buying it from before you decide to spend hard-earned money on it.

	QUALITY OF ANIMALS	COST
BREEDER	A breeder will be able to orient you to the health and status of the animals in their herd or flock. Animals from breeders come with information regarding their bloodline, which allows consumers to have a better idea of what kind of animal they are purchasing.	Naturally, this option will tend to be more expensive. This will likely be the priciest option for purchasing new livestock.
AUCTION	The quality of animals at auction can be suspect. Many producers take their cull animals to auction. If you do decide to purchase an animal from this source, make sure to take a close look at the animals being offered before the auction begins so you have a better idea of what you're getting.	Due to the broad range of quality found at auctions, these animals can be bought at fairly low prices. (This is not always the case, and you must keep in mind that you get what you pay for)
PRIVATE PARTY	Animals from private parties (i.e. farm owners) may not come with paperwork like an animal from a breeder would. However, the benefit of buying from an individual like this is that you can usually take a close look at the animal before buying, and the seller will usually be happy to answer any questions you might have about getting started with your farm.	Falling between auction animals and livestock from certified breeders, this price point is a comfortable middle ground.

AGRITOURISM

Abbe Turner

Agritourism is an important tool for developing revenue streams on small farms. People are looking for an educational and entertaining experience for themselves and their families, and they're willing to pay quite handsomely for it, actually.

Historically, we have seen activities such as apple picking, U-pick grapes, hayrides and more as the small farm is ideally suited for the experience economy. Although starting any new venture as part of a business or a farm has its risks, agritourism is something that can be started on a small scale and grown into something significant for increased farm-based income.

There are three agritourism basics:
1. Have something for visitors to see
2. Have something for visitors to do
3. Have something for visitors to buy

Often, farms are driving customers to their locations with free activities but there are still many opportunities for value-added income to be made, such as selling food, beverages, souvenirs or enhanced ticketed activities.

Agritourism and visits to the farm can often become an annual family experience. Think about the measuring stick against the apple tree as little Billy grows up and then comes back and brings his children to pick apples at the same tree where he was measured. These experiences create a sense of history, tradition and place, making these venues sought-after destinations year after year.

In order to ensure a good experience for farm visitors, as well as earned income for the farmer, the farm not only needs to be aesthetically pleasing but also highly functional to accommodate the activities that are provided, including resting spaces and facilities for all ages in the family.

When you consider the spaces at your farm, think about passive activities such as relaxing or socializing, maybe in your gardens or greenhouses. Also consider active activities such as pony rides, petting zoo, trail walks or square dancing in the barn. You will also need flexible gathering spaces for weddings, concerts, family reunions or other types of special events.

Certain intentionally designed spaces can dramatically increase farm income, for events such as weddings, farm-to-table dinners, large parties or receptions and corporate events. These bigger events also require additional infrastructure, such as increased parking, a tour bus turnaround, handicap accessibility, catering kitchen and storage and even more restrooms. A large tent pad is a significant expense in concrete but can save the day when your client is a bridezilla and bad weather threatens.

At Lucky Penny Farm, we have tried a variety of on-farm events, to both great and limited success. Our first event was an Edible Weeds Workshop where we went foraging in our fields for wild edibles and then cooked lunch from what we collected in our pastures. We certainly did not expect 150 people to show up and I ended up cooking Garlic Mustard Pesto, Lambs Quarter Fritters and Purslane salad for hours on end. Our property had never before or since been so well weeded. We now know to require people to register in advance, preferably with a credit card, rain or shine, no refunds.

Other events included school bus tours, a folk concert, a goat cheese day camp and goat yoga. We have learned from each of these events as we built a following of families who enjoyed coming to Lucky Penny Farm to play with the goats and purchase goat cheese. Many of these visitors went on to become loyal customers, hiring us to do fondue parties, to assemble gift baskets at the holidays or to create cheese boards for their weddings.

HASTINGS DAIRY WAGON RIDE & COW TRAIN

When you do host these on-farm events, be sure to have the appropriate insurance (call your agent and ask for a one-day policy), adequate restroom facilities, and dry parking spaces. At the end of the day, the last thing you want to be doing is pushing cars out of your muddy field. We have heard of experiences where a car gets stuck so they bring in a tractor and then the tractor gets stuck and then the next tractor gets stuck and so on and so on.

On a final note, take a hard look around your farm for things that may be visually unappealing or downright dangerous. We had a lovely educational table of antique farm tools on display, not thinking that a rambunctious child would grab a rusty axe and run. Yikes!! Lesson learned.

Example: Lucky Penny Farm Agritourism Story

Lucky Penny Farm in Garrettsville, Ohio is home to 70 Nubian, La Mancha and Alpine Dairy goats. Owned by Abbe and Anderson Turner since 2002, they have re-established the 14-acre farm according to sustainable agricultural practices, and have expanded the dairy goat herd to include breeds that produce top quality milk, ideal for artisanal cheeses, yogurt and confections. True to artisan standards, the creamery crafts the goat cheeses and candies by hand, in small batches, using only the highest quality milk from Ohio farms.

GOAT YOGA

The Turners perceive an opportunity to educate others about artisan cheeses and dairy goats, sharing their farm story; how they and the many farms they work with raise the animals, protect and enrich the land, make the milk and produce the dairy delights that the community enjoys.

Join us on the farm for a Mother's Day Brunch and guided pasture walk with the goat herd. Reservations required. Appropriate footwear recommended.

CREME BRULEE
FOR MOTHERS DAY

BRENDA HASTINGS

Hastings Dairy & Rowdy Cow Creamery | Burton, OH

Creating an Agribusiness on the Family Farm

I'm Brenda Hastings. My husband, Lad, and I operate Hastings Dairy and Rowdy Cow Creamery, a family-operated dairy farm and farmstead creamery in Burton, Ohio. We have two sons: Garrett (16) and Jack (13). Lad and I started this dairy in 2004 with 500 milk cows. We currently milk over 600 cows, raise all our own replacement heifers, and farm about 700 acres.

I grew up on a dairy farm in Tulare, California and come from several generations of dairy farmers. I graduated from California State University, Fresno with an Ag Business degree and received a master's degree from Cal Poly, San Luis Obispo. After college, I worked for World-Wide Sires in advertising and public relations, then for the University of California-Davis School of Veterinary Medicine in an administrative role. My work brought me to World Dairy Expo where I met Lad in 1995. We were married two years later.

Before starting our own family farm, Lad and I put together a business plan and financial projections to take to the bank for financing. We assembled the plan using our family experience operating a dairy farm, working in the dairy industry and our educational backgrounds in business and agriculture.

Our dairy facility is unique because it has a large meeting room area with a wall of windows that allow visitors to watch the cows milking. Many people are curious about what happens on a dairy farm and have questions about animal care. So in 2011, we added agritourism to our farm, offering tours and providing an event venue for parties. We host several "Milk from Cow to Bottle" tours open to the public and offer private tours for groups of all ages. Our farm is located 45 minutes east of Cleveland, so we draw visitors from surrounding metropolitan areas who are interested in learning about dairy and having a fun family experience.

In 2015, we diversified our farm by adding a small on-farm creamery: Rowdy Cow Creamery. We bottle whole milk in white, chocolate and a variety of other flavors. In 2018, we

BRENDA HASTINGS

started making Fromage Blanc cheese to expand our offerings. In 2019, we plan to add two more varieties of cheese. We deliver these products to local stores and restaurants.

In addition to farming, I believe it's important to do my part in the community and dairy industry. I've served on the American Dairy Association Mideast Board, Ohio Dairy Producers Board, Leadership Geauga Board, am past President of the Geauga County Farm Bureau Board, past President of Burton Elementary PTO, past President of Geauga County Panhellenic, a member of the Geauga County Tourism Council, Geauga County Agricultural Society and Geauga County Historical Society.

Our biggest success is our cows. They are the #1 priority on our farm. Our cows are healthy, productive, well-fed and very comfortable. We're proud of how we operate our farm and care for the animals. At the same time, the #1 challenge on our dairy farm, and many dairy farms, is the economic risk involved. Dairy farming is capital-intensive and takes a large financial investment.

Dairy farming is also a 365-day-per-year job. The cows need to be milked, fed and cared for every day. Dairy farming requires a major commitment of the entire family. If you add a creamery or agritourism or farm market to diversify your farm, it requires even more work and time. Be prepared to pledge the large majority of your time and finances to the business.

THE HASTINGS FAMILY: JACK, GARRETT, BRENDA & LAD

Dairy farming is meaningful and rewarding work, and a good environment to raise a family. Lad and I value raising our sons on a farm because it demonstrates a strong work ethic, commitment, accountability, and provides many life lessons. Our farm, creamery and active boys keep us busy.

This dairy life has its rewards and challenges. We work each day to provide the best for our cows, family, staff and community. We're optimistic about the future of dairy farming and strive to sustain what we've created in order to provide opportunities for future generations.

MICHELLE GORMAN

Integration Acres | Athens County, Ohio

Diversification is Key to Successful Integration

Integration Acres is a multi-faceted agricultural enterprise that includes a farmstead goat dairy, a pawpaw processing facility and a walnut hulling station. The family-owned farm also features an Airbnb rental property. Established in 1996, it has been producing farmstead goat cheese since 2007.

With markets constantly shifting, we've realized that we always need to stay one step ahead, and we've been successful by having a highly diversified farm. We ultimately purchased this property from my husband's parents, and two years ago, we launched the onsite farmhouse as a "farmstay" lodging rental on Airbnb. We also process and freeze pawpaws, serve as a black walnut hulling station, raise whey-fed hogs and support the local food foraging community by purchasing spicebush berries, ramps,

INTEGRATION ACRES

mushrooms and other non-timber forest products. We understood early on that cheesemaking was just one part of Integration Acres, and we've relied on all possible income streams.

We've been successful in building our brand name locally and regionally, and that's largely because Integration Acres is so diversified. We also pay our employees well over minimum wage, which we believe has resulted in a dedicated, diligent and committed staff.

I have a varied background, with a Bachelor of Science degree in Magazine Journalism from Ohio University. Prior

MICHELLE GORMAN
PHOTO CREDIT: BRIAN BLAUSER

to owning and operating Integration Acres, I worked in tourism, marketing and with non-profits. I also serve as a coordinator for the Ohio Pawpaw Festival. My husband, Chris Chmiel, and I live with our two children in a passive solar, rammed earth tire house in rural Athens County, Ohio.

During the early days of Integration Acres, I worked in the local tourism field while my husband developed the farm on a cow dairy that his parents initially had bought as a retirement investment. We decided to transition the pre-existing dairy into a goat milking facility, and eventually added two walk-in coolers, a freezer and another commercial kitchen space. The space became a licensed, inspected cheesemaking facility in 2007. After taking time off while our children were young, I returned to Integration Acres full-time in 2009 as cheesemaker. By 2013, I assumed most of the farm's day-to-day operations, including bookkeeping/payroll, staffing, marketing, maintenance and rental management.

This diversified lifestyle is a challenge! Dairying is challenging, but so is any small business, especially specialty food outfits. It's not always easy to market and sell a higher-end, healthier food product when endless (and cheaper) highly processed foods are so abundant.

My advice to fellow women in agriculture is this: Understand what the market is like in your geographical region. Making cheese is the easy part. Finding places to sell it, and getting it to those places can be a real challenge.

Also, be aware of dairies already operating in your sphere. Depending on your location, the market may or may not be able to support multiple entrepreneurs making the same product. Go through the appropriate channels when it comes to rules and regulations. The Ohio Department of Agriculture is very supportive, and their staff have always provided great consulting advice.

There is so much to be done and you cannot do it alone. Over the years, we have employed women of varying ages, backgrounds and life experiences. Two herd managers (one current and one former) worked at the farm for over five years each. I'd like to believe we've created an environment at Integration Acres where people are empowered to manage and make decisions, feel appreciated and are appropriately compensated.

HOW?

THE BUSINESS PLAN

Abbe Turner

"Be your own boss, love yourself, get up and dance. Your time is now."
- Ciara, Level Up

If the thought of writing a business plan has you shaking in your boots, you are not alone.

The document is significant and an important tool for your success and the strategic direction of your business. But the physical document itself is just words and figures on paper. The great strength of creating a business plan is the experience and education you gain while putting it together.

We went through many versions of our first business plan (a hefty 74 pages), but then we found that when we sat in banks with loan officers, they only looked at three pages: the executive summary, break-even analysis and the income statement. It's so much nicer now that plans are shorter and you are not expected to write a tome about your Tomme.

If this is your first time writing a business plan, I encourage you to start small before you move into a full-fledged plan. Start by answering these questions in a notebook.

Yes, write it down:
1. Describe your business
2. What do you think your startup expenses will be? And your operating expenses?
3. Make a list of how you will make money, your revenue streams
4. What resources do you have currently (skills, physical assets such as real estate, equipment, livestock, professional contacts)

When you write this, imagine that you are talking to your friend. Sometimes it even helps to look at a picture of someone you know when you write. Tell your friend you are hoping to find the right product and use the right system to produce it to be sustainable and profitable.

After you've put those first four questions down on paper, answer these questions:

5. What makes your business unique?
6. Who are your customers?
7. How big is the market?
8. How do you plan to grow your business?
9. Who are you?
10. What do you need to be successful?
11. How much money do you have now?
12. What is your current financial position?

By answering these questions, you will have the appropriate content to fill in the required sections of a formal business plan. I say required, but that's not really quite true, as every plan is different and unique to you and your business. That being said, there are certain elements that a bank or investor will be looking for in your plan.

These include:

An Executive Summary

The Nature of Your Business

The Product

Competitive Analysis

A Marketing Plan

The Management Team

Timetable

Financial Projections

Supporting Information

When you can provide answers to all of these questions and can provide truthful narrative content for all of these sections, you will have the confidence necessary to make your pitch to banks, private investors, or even family members that you might need to sell on the idea of taking the farm, land, cows, insert blank here, in a different direction. Sometimes those people closest to you are the toughest customers.

The longer version of your business plan, if you choose to expand the basic text, will include more narrative about your product or business ecosystems. Each of these sections should be straightforward, short and realistic. Recognize that you really don't know the answer to many of these questions and, in many cases, you may be grabbing numbers out of the air; at least try to make them informed numbers. No one will believe that you're going to sell 10,000 pounds of cheese in your first month, let alone your first year. (The Farmstead Creamery Advisor has a nice, concise description of each element of a plan.)

Sample narrative from the Lucky Penny Business Plan:
There is a new attitude about foods and flavors and a movement towards embracing locally grown and produced foods. Consumers are expressing more distrust and dissatisfaction with large corporations, leading to a desire for simpler, fresher and potentially safer foods sourced locally. These consumers are seeking out farmers markets and grocers that are willing and able to stock such products, including artisan specialty cheeses and gourmet confections.

The word "artisan" or "artisanal" implies that a product is produced primarily by hand, in small batches, with particular attention paid to the art of creation, thus using as little mechanization as possible in the production of the product.

The Lucky Penny Promise:
To provide the highest quality goat cheeses and culinary experiences to our customers while educating them about local, sustainable agriculture.

We will accomplish this by:
- Establishing and maintaining working relationships and contractual agreements with chefs, wholesalers, retailers, distributors, caterers and restaurants.
- Telling the farm story with honesty and integrity and communicating the benefits of artisanal products for direct sales such as freshness, quality and food safety.
- Bringing the new facility (an adaptive re-use of a blighted building) to significant production levels within two years.
- Appropriately measuring and managing all production aspects for continuous improvement to the bottom line.
- Becoming an engine for rural economic development and a model for entrepreneurial agriculture.

Your story will be your own, so start putting it on paper. If you are like me and would much rather be outside mending fences than inside writing, try this exercise. As you work on answering these questions, set a timer for five minutes and try to fill one sheet of paper as fast as you can for each of the following questions. Don't worry about punctuation or grammar or spelling or even if your sentences make sense. Just get them out of your head and put them down on paper. You can edit later. If you need chunks to chew on, make a plan to do one question per day. Just five minutes. You can do it. Start today.

Go:
1. Describe your business.
2. What do you think your startup expenses will be? And your operating expenses?
3. Make a list of how you will make money, your revenue streams.
4. What resources you have currently (skills, physical assets such as real estate, equipment, livestock, professional contacts).
5. What makes your business unique?

Funding Your Plan

There are many sources of money for your business plan. Some are easier to obtain, some should be avoided, and some are unexpected. These include traditional banks, loans, grants, lines of credit, venture capital, private investors, Slow Money groups, crowdfunding, personal savings, credit cards and family members. Look around and consider selling things you don't need. You will need to learn to pare down and live lean as an entrepreneur in your early years, so you might as well lighten your load now and turn your extra stuff into cash. (You won't have time for that boat or vacation home anyway, when you get started...)

Be cautious and careful about how you navigate this part of growing your business. Trust your gut instincts too and walk away from money that you get a bad vibe about, is offered at too high an interest rate, or if someone is overbearing or just plain creepy. There were many times we were flat broke and the temptation and pressure conspired to bring in another investor. But in hindsight, we recognized that person didn't understand us or what we were about, or only wanted our contacts with celebrity chefs.

I may be stating the obvious here, but don't go into business with someone you don't want to spend a lot of time with and don't take money from someone you don't like. Only use credit cards in extreme emergencies, and don't borrow against the house or farm unless you plan on losing them. To this day, I regret liquidating my retirement account. It seemed like a good idea at the time. Be careful to not take on too much debt early on. You can borrow more later on, as your business grows and new pressure cracks develop. You can start small with a limited investment and prove your concept in the marketplace first. Then figure out what your expanding business needs next. First things first.

EXPENSE BREAKDOWN

The chart below represents data that Mintel Research found to be averages of operating expense break downs after interviewing specialty food producers. Ingredients, packaging, and labor make up a large portion of expenses.

INDUSTRY STANDARD

ADMINISTRATIVE (9%)

PACKAGING (12%)

INGREDIENTS (29%)

PRODUCTION/SHIPPING (21%)

OTHER (19%)

MARKETING (10%)

*Data sourced from Mintel Research

The chart below represents one week in season for total revenue and expenses for Lucky Penny Creamery.

LUCKY PENNY CREAMERY

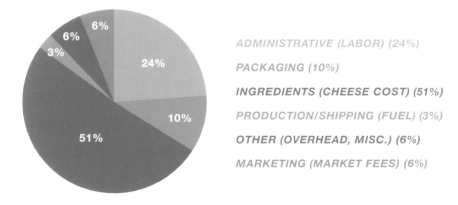

ADMINISTRATIVE (LABOR) (24%)

PACKAGING (10%)

INGREDIENTS (CHEESE COST) (51%)

PRODUCTION/SHIPPING (FUEL) (3%)

OTHER (OVERHEAD, MISC.) (6%)

MARKETING (MARKET FEES) (6%)

BRANDING

Madeline Turner

Insights On Branding Your Artisan Dairy Business

VISION → VALUES → VALUE

Attention to your vision will elevate your brand's value. Unless people are exposed to and identify with your brand and product, you will fail to gain the commercial success you seek. The biggest mistake farmers make when bringing their products into the market is a lack of attention to branding; consumers of artisan dairy aren't just looking for a quality product, they are looking for a quality product that also makes them feel good about buying it. Your brand, therefore, should be informed by your unique values and story.

There are four main tenets you should consider when branding your artisan dairy company: story, community, aesthetics, and social media. Everything should be in harmony with the true you and the truth of your product.

Story

Your story is your success. Why is this the case? You have to intentionally define yourself and your company in order for people to understand why they should buy your products. All of our stories will be different and you should strive to embrace what makes you and your product unique; don't tell a story a certain way because other people are telling it, because as kitschy as it sounds, being able to bring something unique to the marketplace will translate to higher sales than telling the same story over and over again. Practice telling the story of your brand by distilling it to five words that define your brand's personality — this is challenging, but by outlining the core values of your brand, you will be able to translate your story into effective messaging. Tell your story time and time again — just because you're sick of it doesn't mean that your customer has heard it enough.

When communicating your story and brand attributes, don't overlook your employees. Tell them time and time again, in simple, digestible messages. You can't be everywhere to answer all the questions so your staff needs to be educated and informed not only on technical issues but on your brand values. Craft the story, then live up to it.

You are entering this industry for a reason, therefore everything you are building has meaning. Communicate it. Determine your unique selling proposition: what makes you better or different than your competitor? Centralize this idea in the ways you communicate with consumers, and be sure to tell each product's unique story as well. *How did it get to the consumer, from pasture to plate? What sets it apartfrom other products on the scene? Is its name unique? Does it follow a traditional recipe?* These are just samples of questions

ROWDY COW CREAMERY

you could ask yourself or others, but the heart of the matter is your product's ability to speak for itself just as much as you are able to support it with ideas.

Community

This takes consistent effort; a brand needs a name, a face, and an identifier to rally around. Take care to make consumers feel cared about on the market floor and also to feel connected to others through your product; this can be done through t-shirts and stickers or other traditional means, but also through engagement through media and rewards and incentive programs. The most meaningful aspect of building community for your brand is that community incentivizes continued support - if your brand has an excited group of people loyal to it, then they will continue to support your product. Understanding who your customer or customers truly are is key in this pursuit: for Lucky Penny, for example, our primary customers are educated, female head of households who pay some level of attention to what they eat. We're also interested in reaching people that want to buy local because it's good for the environment and supports the local economy — through these values, customers connect with the product. People crave connection with what they buy; they will want to connect with, and therefore support, a local brand which gives them a sense of community. Our secondary customers are chefs, food distributors, caterers, and grocers who want a local product to enhance their local offerings — this requires engaging in a different way, with different messaging. You need to speak with all of your possible audiences in a way they want to be talked to and in a way they understand.

This community extends to your team as well — if your employees and partners are inspired by your story and can tell it well, the strength of your brand will dramatically increase.

Aesthetics

Be unique, but be attentive to each year's specific demands. This means it is increasingly important to do your research, and to continuously reevaluate and even change your stylistic choices. For example, it may be tempting to go with a classic, old-fashioned, homestead style aesthetic for your farmers market materials, but if everyone is doing it or trends find such a style outdated, the aesthetic will fail to serve your purpose.

INTEGRATION ACRES

Don't underestimate the importance of a good logo. Clip art is probably always a bad idea, and if you have the resources, you should hire someone to design it for you. This may sound trite, but your logo is the image you present to the world and the first thing any potential consumer will identify with your brand. You don't want to make a bad first impression, so set a good tone for the quality of your product by presenting it in the best light. Be sure that all elements of what you do resonate in the same harmony as your story; your logo, your farmers booth display, your advertising, and any other presentation you have with the public. Consistency is mandatory, and will make you feel better.

Social media

Four key ideas related to social media presence:
1. Intentional
    - Social media posts and website updates must be entirely intentional. This means clean, clear, direct messaging that encourages consumer participation.
2. Consistent
    - Again, consistency in frequency and style is paramount. An easy way to ensure this at the beginning is to have one point person to handle your social media posts, or otherwise develop a system to maintain consistency in messaging and style.
    - Frequency is important to enable continued visibility of your brand and maintain relationships outside of the grocery store or farmers market. Utilize social media as an additional opportunity to support other community members that you work with such as chefs, caterers, and farmers.

3. Media Heavy
    *   Reserve large amounts of text for big announcements — otherwise, focus on varying photos and videos.
    *   Invest in a decent smartphone — you don't need to spend capital on an HD camera when the tool in your pocket can be properly utilized to fill your needs at start-up.

Ferrum Moraine Farm & Dairy

Est. 2007 . Kent, Ohio

FERRUM MORAINE FARM

4. Crowdfunding
    *   I include this here because if the need should ever arise for you to crowdfund for equipment, a media presence will be key.
    *   Be intentional about when and for what you crowdfund. This may seem like a given, but it may be more beneficial to run a $10,000 Kickstarter for a business-defining piece of equipment than a $2,000 operating expense.
    *   Again, success in crowdfunding will be increased if you have a strong social media presence and many followers and friends prior to launching a crowdfunding campaign. One needs to proceed the other.

THE PITCH

Madeline Turner

Your pitch needs to be concise, complete, and engaging. This is your story; tell it in a way that translates to the best possible outcomes for your company by centering clarity and appeal to the things that make people happy.

Here are the key aspects of a successful pitch:

Introduction
- This doesn't need to be your life story, rather a short and sweet introduction to who you and your company are.
- Who are your teammates that make what you are doing work?
- What hole do you uniquely fill in the market? What problem does your product address?

Product
- Here, tell us about your unique product. Where does the milk come from? Is there a special name or inspiration? Flavor notes?
- This is where you get to highlight why your product is the way it is.

Traction
- This should be something quantifiable that demonstrates who is your customer base.
- This is proof of the potential of you and your company.

Market
- What does the market look like?
- How big is it?
- Who are your competitors? What makes your goals different from their goals?

Business Model
- Revenue Model
- How are you going to make money?

Ask
- What do you need? Give a specific ask.
- What project do you strategically need to fund to propel your business forward?
- How do you plan to immediately follow your ask with action?

- Examples:
  - I am looking for your store to carry our complete line of 4 seasonal cheese flavors (whatever product you are selling).
  - I am looking for your investment of $10,000 by March 1 to be part of our exciting growth. To what address can I send the documents for your review?
  - I would be grateful for your introduction to Mr. Bob Smith, head of the XYZ venture capital group. Would it be helpful if I sent to you background information about our company?

The goal of your pitch should be to successfully sell your company to whoever is listening regardless of their background in your industry or the business world. The work lies in appealing to people emotionally and in telling a compelling story about why what you are doing is meaningful.

ANGEL KING

Blue Jacket Dairy | Bellefontaine, OH

Finding Balance — Not Burning the Candle at Both Ends

I am Angel King, co-owner of Blue Jacket Dairy with my husband, Jim. Located in Bellefontaine, Blue Jacket is Ohio's leading producer of fresh artisan cheese. But that was not always the case.

So many things go into the decision to launch a value-added dairy business. In our case, the roller-coaster of volatile, fluid milk pricing had reached the point in 2006 that a major decision had to be made.

My husband, a fourth-generation dairy farmer, and I were faced with the reality that it was either necessary to significantly increase the size of the milking operation or create a value-added dairy product. Drawing from my entrepreneurial background in the technology industry, the idea of taking risks to create a new venture was not a scary proposition to me. Much research ensued, and we drafted a business plan to start an artisan cheese business.

After two years of the dream-to-reality phase, Blue Jacket Dairy was launched in 2008. Along the way, it became evident that making cheese is just one facet of the business. Another large facet is the sales and marketing of the product. We quickly learned that selling our cheese is a lot of hard work. The adage, "If you build it, they will come," is not a truism – due to the fact that sales and marketing is a significant piece of the time spent in the business. Hours and hours of time have been — and continue to be — spent on gleaning ideas and determining the best way to promote and sell our cheese.

One of the key things we learned along the way is that no business is immune from the norms of intense hard work, no guarantee of profit, necessary personal passion and constant penny-pinching. All are imperative in order to succeed. Reading books of and by great business leaders has helped us acquire information on the patterns and ideas needed in order to run a profitable business.

Selling a value-added dairy product in retail stores means that the packaging and labeling of the item need to match the particular setting. It should jump out at the customer and grab their attention since it's competing with other products on the shelves. Of particular importance is having a UPC on the package. Also, in-store demos are a fantastic way to introduce the product to new customers.

Our sales channels have been numerous, ranging from farmers markets, direct-to-store, on-site, distributors, mail order and food service. While each sales channel is an important piece of our business, we have found it critical to regularly evaluate our sales reports for trends in our business. At one point, we were attending 20 farmers markets each week. Exciting as it was to be a part of a large number of farmers markets over the years, we found it necessary to adjust which markets we attended each year, based on our sales data and trends. Limited resources of time and staffing require matching those resources appropriately. Over time, where we initially had a higher percentage of sales in the farmers market channel, it has been replaced by sales in the food service industry.

One of the biggest personal challenges for me in running a small food-production business is making sure to find balance in my life. The goal of the business is to make

ANGEL & JIM, BLUE JACKET DAIRY

money, but not at the expense of my marriage, family, health or friendships. It has been a journey to figure out this balance, but several things have helped me to accomplish this. Realizing that each business needs a team of people, I am more effective in my efforts when surrounded by a strong team to whom tasks can be confidently delegated to on a regular basis.

The second thing has been to establish work hours. As an owner, I have found that the business will consume all the hours it is given. So, by creating a boundary of reasonable start and stop times, I am left with space for a balanced life. I am far more efficient at Blue Jacket Dairy when I am not burning the candle at both ends.

HULL'S TRACE

MARKETING

Abbe Turner

No matter how wonderful your product is, without sales, it goes nowhere and does nothing to build your brand or put money in the bank. You have consumers who are the end users of your product and customers in the form of distributors or retailers who put your product in the marketplace. It's important that you understand what both of these types of purchasers are looking for regarding quality, packaging, delivery, certifications, pricing and story. Take the time to research and understand the market, what products are selling and any competitive companies. Then be sure to highlight your unique selling proposition or what makes your cheese unique or different from the others.

For Lucky Penny, the purchase decision for our customer is based on integrity and trust in our quality, safety, traditional recipes, grazing practices and animal husbandry. The Lucky Penny brand means that the product has been handcrafted and prepared with the best ingredients, delivering the best flavors produced from the milk of goats on grass. Our dairy products and candies may be priced higher than similar products in the market because of our premium placed on quality. Our customers and end consumers are willing to pay more for our product because they know us through our community involvement and they trust in our brand. They also may resonate with our values and philosophies regarding sustainable farming, Slow Money and Slow Food.

Advertising, whether traditional or non-traditional on social media, promotional campaigns and in-store sampling, are all strong ways to raise awareness and sales of your products in the marketplace. I cannot overstate the power of sampling and demos to sell products.

The best way for someone to truly understand what your company stands for is to have them taste your good, clean dairy products. (When sampling, be sure to account for the product distributed in your advertising budget and track the quantities accordingly.)

When scheduling in-store sampling, the highest driver to success is the person doing the selling. Your brand ambassador should look the part, speak with enthusiasm, be knowledgeable and also be able to answer questions about methods of production, product attributes, and even share farm stories with those interested. *And they are interested.* (Sometimes people are too interested and you miss talking to 10 potential customers because the person in front of you is sharing their story of when they had their first goat. This happens too often, really. Move them on graciously, with a smile.)

It is also helpful to have attractive and well-designed sales literature to distribute. Some stores allow couponing but I have not seen that build long-term sales. Often your short-term reward is just a one-off purchase and people who are buying on price might not necessarily be your target customer.

A simple postcard including a recipe for suggested product use is a nice handout. At Lucky Penny, we distributed a Chevre cookie recipe card and one of the unintended side effects was that people often brought their version of the cookie to me at farmers markets, always a welcome surprise. I rewarded them with free cheese and a loyalty card, compliments of the cheesemaker.

Speaking of loyalty cards, they are another way to build increased sales (Buy 8 cheeses; get 1 free!) and although tough to do at a retailer, this is a wonderful way to capture dollars at the farmers market. Customers love the promotion and we love their repeat sales. If you have an unlimited printing and design budget, I also recommend tent cards for restaurants, posters for your retailers and shelf talkers for the grocery stores. There also can be small cards that act as product information tags, tied around the product with a string. These can be used for any kind of promotional information: your story, ingredients, certifications, company history, cute animal pictures or to send away for a free T-shirt. The benefit of these printed mechanisms is that they are already affixed to the product and don't require the retailer to do any additional work. For retailers, any additional steps are frowned upon (and often are never executed), as store personnel are already overwhelmed with their daily responsibilities and have to listen, half-heartedly, to that customer telling the story about her first goat. I'm not kidding; pardon the pun.

Regarding all marketing materials, a talented designer is a very important part of your team and well worth the investment as you build your brand and try to capture a bigger piece of the market share. Outsource this early and often and let the professionals do their work while you do what you're good at: raising cows, making cheese. (For printing paper goods, my first choice is to recommend Jakprints in Cleveland (jakprints. com.) For labels, I use Stand Out Stickers (standoutstickers.com), far and away the best and most durable stickers for refrigerated products. Use the word "milk" in the promo code spot for an automatic 15% discount. Everything counts.

As your company grows and you continue to market your cheese, it's important to determine how big you want your geographic reach to be. Are you a local-only company, regional or trying to build a national brand? And are you consistently producing enough cheese to serve these expanded markets? No chef likes to be told that your product is sold out. To protect your regular loyal clientele, you need to be in stock all the time, the exception being during seasonal fluctuations in lactation. Train your customers to appreciate that fluctuations in milk supply reflect how close they are to the farm and the seasons when purchasing your product. Make this an appealing part of your story; not an obstacle.

Shipping

How will you get the cheese to the customers? Will this be a direct sale or direct delivery (be sure to charge a nominal fee) or will you ship by UPS or FedEx? An obvious challenge is that certain dairy products must be shipped cold and maintained at that temperature to protect product integrity. Many times, the combined cost of packaging and shipping is higher than the total cost of the cheese being shipped. These are costs that you pass on to the customer, as in most cases if you don't then you would be operating at a loss.

Working with Chefs

At Lucky Penny, we've been very lucky to work with a strong community of chefs across Ohio. We have built this to be a major portion of our business by understanding their businesses and providing to them what they want when they want it. We work with chefs to educate their entire kitchen staff about the uniqueness of our cheeses and the best way to manage their care on the line. We have hosted chef dinners (yes, dinners for chefs!) on Monday evenings (their day off) at the farm, where they could meet the animals, walk the pastures, visit the creamery and learn more about our farm story. We readily respond to requests for information, we deliver quickly when receiving orders, we allow tours at any time and we provide a heavy sampling budget so the chefs can test our products in their recipes prior to making the commitment to buy. We also ask the chefs for their honest opinions as to ways to improve our product or its functionality in their restaurant kitchen and we contact them when they want to be contacted, between 2pm and 4pm only; in many cases, on a set day by text only. This respect helps to foster strong, long-term relationships and loyal, repeat customers.

EVERYONE LOVES COOKIES!

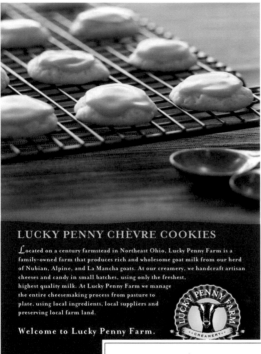

LUCKY PENNY CHÈVRE COOKIES

*L*ocated on a century farmstead in Northeast Ohio, Lucky Penny Farm is a family-owned farm that produces rich and wholesome goat milk from our herd of Nubian, Alpine, and La Mancha goats. At our creamery, we handcraft artisan cheeses and candy in small batches, using only the freshest, highest quality milk. At Lucky Penny Farm we manage the entire cheesemaking process from pasture to plate, using local ingredients, local suppliers and preserving local farm land.

Welcome to Lucky Penny Farm.

LUCKY PENNY CHÈVRE COOKIES

These cookies are based on Italian ricotta cookies. They are cakey and light, and made without eggs. They are also quick to make and you can get the whole family involved. They are wonderful with chocolate, orange or lemon icing, and increase the citrus flavor by adding the zest of one orange or lemon to the batter. Use your imagination!

For the cookies:
½ cup unsalted butter, softened
1 cup granulated sugar
8 oz. soft goat cheese (chèvre)
¼ cup milk
2 tsp. vanilla
⅛ tsp. salt
½ tsp. baking soda
2 cups all-purpose flour

For the icing:
½ cup powdered sugar
Orange juice
Sprinkles or colored sugar

Preheat the oven to 350 degrees. Mix all cookie ingredients together until the dough comes together into a ball. The dough will be sticky. Place teaspoon-sized balls on ungreased baking sheet, about 2 inches apart. Bake for about 12 minutes or until the bottoms are brown. Let cool for one minute on the baking sheet, and then remove to a rack to cool completely.

In a small saucepan, combine the powdered sugar with enough orange juice to make a glaze to spread on the cookies (a couple of tablespoons or so). Stir over low heat until smooth and glossy, then spread over the cookies. Quickly top with sprinkles or colored sugar. Makes approximately 3-dozen cookies.

LUCKY PENNY FARM
330-572-7550 creamery
www.luckypennyfarm.com

photography: Lauren Parsells 2009

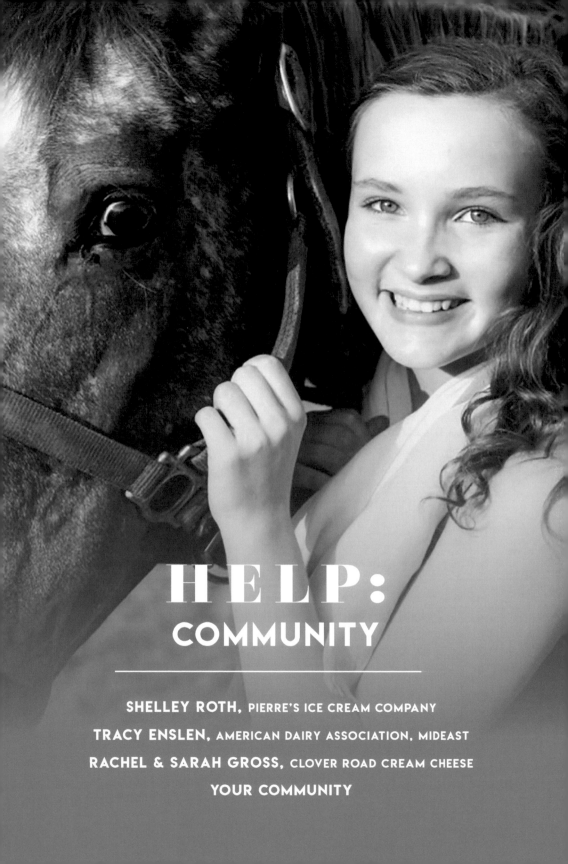

HELP:
COMMUNITY

SHELLEY ROTH, PIERRE'S ICE CREAM COMPANY

TRACY ENSLEN, AMERICAN DAIRY ASSOCIATION, MIDEAST

RACHEL & SARAH GROSS, CLOVER ROAD CREAM CHEESE

YOUR COMMUNITY

SHELLEY ROTH

Pierre's Ice Cream | Cleveland, OH

Keeping a Family-Owned Ice Cream Company Fresh for 87 Years

Shelley Roth is President of Pierre's Ice Cream Company, an 87-year-old regional ice cream manufacturer and distributor. Privately held and family-owned since 1932, Pierre's products are sold throughout Ohio, several other states, and China.

The company also manufactures private label lines for several local and national retail chains and distributes many national brands of ice cream. Since 1932, Pierre's has remained in the heart of Cleveland, with its original, classic recipes as daily reminders of the company's dedication to quality.

Pierre's assortment of products has grown through the years, with over 235 different products/flavors that currently bear the Pierre's name. This dedication influences the company's focus on the future as Shelley guides its development of new opportunities and innovations that align with consumers' changing needs.

Active in numerous community organizations, Shelley also supports the revitalization of Cleveland's neighborhoods in many ways. Over the past 25 years, Pierre's has invested in new buildings for its production, distribution and headquarters on an 8-acre brownfield site at E. 65th and Euclid Avenue. These investments have sustained the company's operation while demonstrating Pierre's commitment and leadership in revitalization and redevelopment of a once-blighted urban neighborhood.

In addition to economic development, the company is engaged in important community works within the region, especially education, with their involvement at the Cuyahoga Community College Foundation. Pierre's supports other charitable causes, including partnership with Vocational Guidance Services, support of local area food banks and contributions toward sustainability.

Shelley received a B.B.A. degree from the University of Michigan. She is also a graduate of Leadership Cleveland. In 1989 and 1990, she served as chairman of the Mid-

SHELLEY ROTH

Town Corridor. She has served on the board of directors of the Cuyahoga Community College Foundation since 1996 and chaired that board from 2004 – 2006. Presently, Shelley serves on the boards of the Rock & Roll Hall of Fame, Cuyahoga Community College Foundation and the International Ice Cream Association. Shelley and her husband, Bruce Schwartz, live in Shaker Heights.

Shelley says the company's greatest successes include "working with a team that is dedicated to quality, safety and service; and contributing to the redevelopment of Midtown Cleveland through our actions to remain in the neighborhood back in the 1990s. Our decision to develop an 8-acre site in a once-blighted area inspired other companies to also invest in the area and turn it into a vibrant neighborhood."

As a relatively small company, Shelley says, "at times it is challenging to incorporate all of the regulations that have emerged. We are particularly pressured at the moment relative to the relabeling of all of our packaging. It is a monumental task and expense, due to the large number of retail products that we produce and our small size relative to other food companies."

One of the first ice cream producers in the country to achieve SQF Level 3000, the highest level of food safety and food quality certification, Pierre's is poised to continue contributing and innovating in the food industry.

PIERRE'S ICE CREAM

Pierre's strives to exceed its customers' expectations by providing the very best products and services ... and works hard to create a challenging and rewarding environment that encourages learning and growth for all of its associates.

Shelley has some advice for women entering the dairy industry: "If you enjoy learning, a career in dairy offers endless opportunities. Dairy touches many aspects of life – whether it relates to food, nutrition, marketing, sales, engineering, production, safety, agriculture, sustainability, or accounting and finance. Don't hesitate to ask for more responsibility or volunteer to be included in projects that will broaden your knowledge, understanding and ultimate contributions to the business."

TRACY ENSLEN

American Dairy Assoc. Mideast & Ohio Cheese Guild | Columbus, OH

Tracy Enslen has a history in dairy. Her young years were influenced by visits to her uncle's dairy farm in Michigan. Her love of cheese was further nurtured during her first job in the cheese shop at Hickory Farms.

Tracy continues to advocate for dairy. She has been promoting the sale of dairy products in Ohio for the past 16 years, working for the American Dairy Association Mideast, the local dairy promotion checkoff program for dairy farmers in Ohio and West Virginia. The association works on behalf of dairy farmers to increase sales and demand of U.S. dairy products and ingredients.

She oversees relationships with milk, cheese and yogurt manufacturers to provide communication, insights and innovation to all cow milk processors, retail and foodservice channels. She also understands the importance of empowering women to follow their ambitions and make them a reality. She focuses on encouraging and locating resources to make the processes easier.

Currently, Tracy also serves on the board of directors for the Ohio Cheese Guild, a non-profit organization dedicated to the support and encouragement of the Ohio cheesemaking community through education and food safety. The OCG is a pre-competitive forum that leverages the collective power of the Ohio cheese community to address the changing needs and expectations of consumers through a framework of shared best practices and accountability. All are welcome, from the cheese enthusiast to foodservice, retail and hobby interests. They all come together for the love of cheese.

TRACY ENSLEN

Speaking about her efforts through the Cheese Guild and Dairy Association, Tracy says, "We are stronger together. When we lift each other up and provide support, we all become better."

She lives with her husband of 20 years, has three adult children and three Dachshund fur babies. When not immersed in dairy, she enjoys hiking, camping and enjoying food experiences.

SARAH & RACHEL GROSS

Clover Road Cream Cheese | Bialy's Bagels in University Hts.

Have you ever heard of "The Schmear Sisters?" If you haven't met them yet, chances are, you have enjoyed the cream cheeses or bagels created by Sarah and Rachel Gross of South Euclid, Ohio. They are the co-creators of Clover Road Cream Cheese launched in 2014 in Kent. They are also co-owners of Bialy's Bagels in University Heights, having taken over the 51-year-old establishment in 2018.

Their cream cheeses mix fresh, local ingredients with creative flavor combinations, handcrafted in small batches from preservative-free milks and creams produced by grass-fed cows. Flavors such as Cinnamon, Sugar & Cayenne; Espresso, Espresso; and Parmesan & Truffle certainly deserved to be paired with the best bagels in town. But how did these 30-something sisters manage such a fast track to success as both cheesemakers and bagel shop owners?

In large part, they owe their rise to their shrewd decision to avoid over-investing capital early on. Since they were new to cheesemaking and new to entrepreneurship, the Gross sisters took their late-night kitchen cream cheese recipes to Abbe Turner, the cheesemaker at Lucky Penny Creamery in Kent. After meeting Abbe through a chance connection, the Grosses decided to partner with Lucky Penny to launch Clover Road Cream Cheese, working side by side with Abbe to learn the ins and outs of perfecting the craft.

Getting mentored in another woman-owned micro dairy incubator allowed Sarah and Rachel to test their product's marketability before investing in their own facility or changing course. In addition to providing use of her facility, Abbe lent her expertise in producing artisan cheeses. She also coordinated recipe development consultation with Snowville Creamery, which now supplies all of Clover Road Cream Cheese's milk and cream.

During the five-day cheesemaking process, the fresh milk and cream undergo pasteurization and culturing before being hand-ladled into cloths for straining. Once finished, one of Clover Road's eight flavor combinations is mixed into the batch, which is then packaged for individual sale.

SARAH & RACHEL GROSS

Clover Road's partnerships with Snowville and Lucky Penny allow the Schmear Sisters to stand by their company's mission: "Spreading our love for fresh food, family and community with creative flavors that are exciting and downright delicious." It also freed them to pursue their initial dream to own and operate a bagel shop. Clover Road Cream Cheese was their first stop along that path.

The Gross sisters like to say that "Clover Road Cream Cheese was born out of a series of happy, delicious experiments." It all started in 2012 when they spent six weeks working at their uncle's bagel shop in North Carolina. This inspired their dream to open their own shop in Ohio. While they waited for that opportunity, they both started working at a northeast Ohio specialty ice cream shop to get the necessary food service industry experience they needed for running their own establishment.

One thing led to the other, and their series of happy, delicious experiments led to fortuitous alliances with Lucky Penny Creamery and Snowville Creamery. In similar fashion, they formed an alliance with Ellen and Mark Osolin of Bialy's Bagels at the time the Osolins decided to retire. They worked closely with the Osolins to make the transition to full ownership within months.

As Bialy's evolves into a third generation of owners, Rachel and Sarah plan to start selling sandwiches at the bagel shop. The two are also developing a new line of coffee called Buster's Brews, working with Brecksville-based Caruso's Coffee Roasters. By 2020, they hope to resume production of Clover Road Cream Cheese, which has been on hiatus since the twins shifted their focus to the bagel shop. They look forward to serving Bialy's Bagels with Clover Road Cream Cheese.

By establishing alliances with trusted masters in their respective fields, the Gross twins have established a winning pattern that serves them well. Their entrepreneurial trajectory continues to expand and onward and upward, with delicious results.

YOUR COMMUNITY

Abbe Turner

At Lucky Penny, we aim to work in harmony with nature as well as within our business ecosystem.

Through our work, we hope to promote sustainable agriculture, protect and preserve traditional recipes and methods of production, protect genetic diversity and the celebration of flavor through our work with heritage breeds, and promote a philosophy that transforms and nurtures our community. We support local nonprofits and community activities, foster growth and personal development in young entrepreneurs and female farmers, and educate the public about the importance of local food to healthy, resilient economies and food systems.

Philanthropy and community involvement have always been priorities at Lucky Penny. We contribute sponsorship support (and lots of cheese!) to green initiatives and events in the arts, social services, hunger and homeless initiatives, conservation and environmental efforts. We also teach cheesemaking workshops, welcome speaking engagements, provide educational programs and agri-tourism events, and support 4-H in our county. The goal is to be a community leader engaging the public in meaningful ways to promote an agriculture we can all live with, in harmony.

Our involvement with community, networking and educational groups is also invaluable, including OEFFA (Ohio Ecological Food and Farm Association), Slow Food, Ohio Cheese Guild, Earth Angel Farms and local libraries. Each of these provides fertile ground for new ideas, business relationships, friendships and support. We need more of all of these.

BLUE JACKET DAIRY

This is a lot to juggle, and in consideration of the pressures on our precious resource of time on a small business, these activities consume a large part of every week. But in truth, it is the most important thing we do: showing up, being present. Take to time lead, take the time to teach, take the time to learn and take the time to help others. And be kind; it is a small community.

Life is funny. As I write this, I hear a goat complaining loudly. It sounds as if she might be stuck in the fence again (always the same goat, Sprout, and always the same spot) and it smells like there is a something burning on the stove and the alarm just went off on my phone to remind me that I have 15 minutes to get to a high school band concert. I should probably comb my hair (first time today) and put on a coat of lipstick. Maybe clean jeans, too.

There is time for everything if you stop and breathe and prioritize. I will start with the stove, rescue the goat, change to clean clothes, then mom it.

HOME

REBECCA ORAVETS, OLD FORGE DAIRY

HEART, HANDS AND HOME: GROWING UP IN ARTISAN DAIRY

CHEESE, LOVE AND BOOTS

REBECCA ORAVETS

Old Forge Dairy, LLC | Kent, OH

Going Green at Old Forge Dairy

Old Forge Dairy, LLC is a husband-and-wife (plus two little kids!) small-scale dairy and farmstead cheese business in Kent, Ohio (Rootstown Township), owned and operated by 28-year-old Rebecca Oravets and her husband, John. They transform the milk from their small herd of Ayrshire cows into a variety of aged, raw milk and natural rind cheeses that have been aged on beechwood boards cut from their stand of woods. Rebecca calls Old Forge "a very green small business — milking eight cows regularly, but we have room to expand if we see fit."

Rebecca was raised on the farm, making her a fifth-generation Winkler to work it, "but it hasn't been a dairy farm since my great-grandparents ran it and we wanted to get back to that," she explains. "There is no practice like dairy farming for building up the permanent fertility of the farm. Dairying is a wonderful way to be a sustainable farmer and it's what our farm is best suited to."

Rebecca spent many years participating in Portage County horse 4-H, attended Rootstown schools and received her BS from Kent State University. She met John when she was just 16 (he was 18) while working at his family's horse farm. They married right after college and bought a fixer-upper home. Rebecca helped with starting her husband's farrier business for a few years (the anvil in their logo speaks to that part of their life as well as the name of their road).

Rebecca recalls, "While living in our small fixer-upper, we managed to have a large garden, raised chickens and pigs, and bought a 'family cow' that started it all. The cow, Joy, was truly my husband's doing, but the cows (and calves) quickly grew on me, and our cow numbers grew too, pushing us to want to make more of our hobby. (Side note: we still have Joy in our herd and she is 12 years old!)"

When the young couple decided to buy Rebecca's parents' portion of the original Winkler farm, they knew they wanted a dairy herd, despite all the advice against it. "The

THE ORAVETS FAMILY:
REBECCA, JUNIOR, MYLA, JOHN P.

biggest decision we had to make was just what kind of business to make of it… Would there be any money in wholesale milk or even someone to pick it up?"

The choices were many: raw milk herdshares, ice cream, or bottling their own milk. Each presented its own set of challenges, and the Oravetses had a lot to lose if they chose the wrong option. "When we finally settled on cheesemaking, we knew it would probably be the most difficult and longest road to get to where we want to be (and we're not there yet!), but it also presented the most demanding and potentially rewarding option," Rebecca says.

Rebecca and John began in late 2015 by working on their old barn and broke ground on their cheese house in December of 2016. Their two little kids — John Paul "Junior" (4) and Myla (1) have been right alongside their parents, building, milking and farming. Rebecca admits, "If that isn't a benefit and challenge rolled up into one, I don't know what is!"

The Oravetses make roughly 45 acres of hay and grow a portion of the grain for their animals. They use a team of Belgian draft horses for much of the farm work, as well as a couple of antique tractors (including Rebecca's great-grandfather's WD, the very first tractor ever used on this farm).

They made their first official batch of cheese in December 2017 and began selling by midsummer 2018. "We have been lucky enough to be welcomed and well received by many local retailers and our community, especially at farmers markets."

Rebecca continues, "Most people would agree that being a mom is hard, thankless, never-ending, yet rewarding work. I think the same can be said for dairy farmers, tied to the animals that we love, and still, the same is true for the cheesemaker, putting in long hours, basically washing things repeatedly and coupled to a craft that is intensely interesting and confusing, with usually very delicious rewards."

Additional challenges are part of the mix: managing workload/time, making a product today that won't be ready for months, difficulty in judging what you are doing right or wrong, trying to predict what types of cheese will store and sell the best, pricing and marketing.

Producing their own milk supply entails a huge amount of demanding work, but Rebecca says it's something they wouldn't change, "because the cows are really the reason we got into cheesemaking in the first place."

HEART, HANDS, AND HOME: GROWING UP IN ARTISAN DAIRY

Madeline Turner

Nothing says "home" to me quite like the pastures adjacent to the farmhouse where I grew up. More than the physical house or the small town up the road, my concept of home (and to some extent, concept of self) has been defined, tested, and shaped by experiences in the barn or in the field. My name is Madeline, and I write this as a 19-year-old child of agriculture, artisan dairy and art — everything I am and will do is, in part, crafted by the beauty of agriculture and the realities of small food business.

Learning occurs in unanticipated ways when every day brings something new. Out of my childhood comes a deep-rooted appreciation for the land, and beyond that, an ability to connect to and with other people through it, no matter where I plant my feet. Being a farm kid, I have always been acutely aware of cycles of life and death — as someone who has delivered hundreds of "kids" or baby goats, to the world, I know exactly the power a second has. I have raised animals and I've decided which animals to send to slaughter. I've been there for animal death and my goats or horses have been present for some of the happiest moments of my life. Children of the industry, like me, have a deeper respect for and connection with what it means to be alive.

Living as a child within a small family business also carries a unique weight. For as long as I can remember, I have had an acute awareness of the impact of a single dollar. There are things that can't be hidden from a child, and perhaps they shouldn't be. In the process of considering what to include in this project, we found business plans I wrote at the age of 9 that focused heavily on an ability to make a profit. I knew that my family was pouring all of their money into the business, and could feel the irreparable stress it put on them. This makes you thrifty and cautious and transforms your relationship with money. That being said, the skills I have learned through the industry have transformed my path and continue to facilitate my future. From the age of 8 on, I knew how to close a sale on the ground at the farmers' market, even though it was initially imperfect. At the risk of sounding overconfident, I can sell anything to anyone now. The skills in sales and interpersonal communications I learned through my family's business have served me well, and have been transformed into a love for entrepreneurship and socially-responsible business.

MADELINE AND TOBY

Children hear everything, and even if they don't hear, they are uniquely capable of feeling what is going on around them. My parents' marriage didn't make it out of the last 10 years in the industry. But no matter the hardships, we all grew exponentially and became closer in so many ways. I know, at the end of the day, I am who I am because of the farm I grew up on and the unique ways small business transformed the course of my family and life. No matter the past or future outcomes, I feel an overwhelming sense of pride in what my family has created, and such deep love for the industry that continues to engage me in ways I never anticipate. This life has taught me the beauty of transformation and evolution — I cannot wait to see what tomorrow brings.

CHEESE, LOVE, AND BOOTS

Abbe Turner

"When you love what you do, you will discover the power in what it means to do it well. Before you know it, people will seek you out, share in your dreams and help you in ways you never imagined."
- Lisa Kivirist, Ecopreneuring

The best-laid business plan will not prepare you for the unexpected that arises over the course of running a food- or farm-based business. At Lucky Penny, we had 14 versions of a business plan that we worked on with multiple economic development agencies, but reality is another thing. The actual business looked nothing like what we had planned. While the costs were high, so were the damages we could not measure until too late. The financial and emotional pressures on the family were greater than expected and often intolerable. I made mistakes and put my energies in the wrong buckets. When my now former husband told me that I abandoned the family by working 90-hour weeks, it hurt, but sometimes he was right. It was an ugly time. "Things change, things evolve and things erupt," says Kivirist.

The constant pressures pushed the family beyond everyone's comfort zone: The electricity got turned off, mental health was challenged, threats of the farm foreclosing loomed, forcing family members to dig deep in their pockets again (thank you, Barbara). Ridiculous lawsuits had to be defended which fractured the focus of the business's true mission and each negative experience frayed the family fabric. Things began to fall apart as the business consumed more resources of mom, money and time; more than what was in the bank, emotionally and financially. Sometimes, in our quest to be everything, it leaves us with nothing. There is no happy ending, yet there are many productive days of joy and fulfillment interspersed with days when I just want to light a match. I believe this is normal.

My best guess is that part of the answer is in the word "Slow." Slow Food, Slow Money and Slow Down. The book Ecopreneuring suggests using their DQLI: A Diversified Quality of Life Index to slow the pace of life. I encourage visiting and revisiting these ideas with your family as well as your team. The DQLI considers various factors, including the health of family relationships, enjoyment of work, physical health and well-being, level of satisfaction with life, and opportunities for continued development.

The central tenets of DQLI:
- Having a meaningful livelihood that expresses our passion, creativity and soul.
- Ongoing opportunities for lifelong learning and experiences.
- Maintaining mental, physical and holistic spiritual health.
- Opportunities for continuous personal, spiritual and creative development.
- Having control over our schedules.
- Building solid, meaningful relationships with our family and friends.
- The satisfaction and joy that comes with greater self-sufficiency.
- Connecting to the interdependent Web of Life that provides an abundance of diverse perspectives and experiences.

The goal of any socially conscious entrepreneur is to create value from their values and to make a life, not just a living. By slowing down, we enjoy the moment, focus and reduce anxiety. It almost seems counterintuitive to talk about Slow activities when considering the hectic, frazzled, frenetic pace of the day-in, day-out routine of a small business. However, that is exactly why slowing down matters. It helps us become more flexible, composed, loving and resilient as we grow our families and our businesses simultaneously.

The tenacity and grit of the women's stories shared in this book put me in awe of what each of them has accomplished. As you begin your food or farm venture, remember that we, as a community of women in dairy, are here to help you succeed in your enterprise. I share with you the answer I gave a new cheesemaker who asked me the question, "When will it get easier?" I told her, "For me, it hasn't gotten easier, but it has always been wonderful. It doesn't involve pantyhose, either. To me, that's always a plus. I much prefer to wear boots."

ENTREPRENEURIAL TENETS

LUCKY PENNY FARM

Slay your dragons.

Build your rocket.

Yes, you can!

Make your soul glow.

Tailspin is temporary.

Cut off the bad fruit.

Make a mess.

Serve your community.

Give it 24 hours.

Failure is inevitable. So fail, then get back up.

Go out on a limb.

Today's the beginning.

Everything counts.

*Just because no one's done it this way
before is no reason not to do it.*

Let it flow.

WITH GRATITUDE

From Abbe

This book would not have been possible without the vision of Rural Action and the funding from NCR-SARE. Thank you for allowing me this opportunity to share the Lucky Penny story with others.

Thank you to Madeline Turner, Amber Sattelberg, Estelle Brown, and Cara Piombo for doing the heavy lifting. Each of these beautiful women carried the load.

Thank you to Tracy Enslen, Ed Burke, Julie Grant and Christine Dodd for your good thinking and constant encouragement.

Thanks also to our Slow Money friends, investors and chefs, especially Karen Small at Flying Fig, who made the story possible.

Full appreciation goes to Russ Vernon at West Point Market for always setting me on the right course and assuring me I wasn't alone.

Thank you to those strong and capable women who took time away from their families, farms, and businesses to share their stories. I have learned valuable insight from all of you. Namaste.

I extend gratitude to those in the industry who took my neophyte calls and requests for meetings to discuss starting this crazy business: Peter Dixon, Allison Hooper at Vermont Creamery, Judy Schad at Capriole Goat Cheese, Anne Hauser, Dee Harley at Harley Farms, Tom and Nancy Clark at Old Chatham, and Ari Weinzweig at Zingerman's. I promise to pay the time you spent with me forward.

Thank you to Tami Mitchell for always keeping a chilled Gruner Veltliner.

Hats off to my wonderful goat herd at Lucky Penny Farm: Cocoa, Trixie, Blackie, Sasquatch, Toast, Sprout, Raspberry Beret, Eggplant, Dart, Georgie and Frankie. You make me happy even on the most difficult of days.

Thank you to Anderson Turner for always believing and making the dream possible.

Deep gratitude to my children: Madeline, Lily and Ezra, for your resilience and loving energy every day. You are the source of my greatest joy and happiness. I am proud to be your mom.

Thank you to Warren Taylor, the original Dairy Evangelist and my favorite milkman.

Final thanks to Mom and Dad for always celebrating my tenacity and never putting out the flame.

WITH GRATITUDE

From Madeline

With gratitude and acknowledgement to the stolen land we write about, the land where all of the farms and creameries written about exist on, which belongs to the Erie, Miami, Potawatomi, Osage, Peoria, and Shawnee Peoples. May we continue to acknowledge the impact of our presence and work to undo the pain we have caused this land and its stewards.

With gratitude to the Smith Startup Consulting Team for their support, education, and recommendations.

With gratitude to all of the folks who worked on this project -- it has been such a dream to be on this team.

With gratitude to all of my wonderful friends for all of their excitement and support -- thank you, especially, to Julie for editing my pieces and to Ella and Julia for keeping me grounded.

With gratitude to my families both chosen and biological, and all of the people who make it so beautiful -- Lily and Ezra, thanks for always being along for the ride.

With gratitude to my goats, my greatest teachers. Eggplant, I miss you so much when I'm not with you.

THANKS & RURAL ACTION STORY

We would like to thank our friends at Rural Action who supported the idea of this book and helped to produce *The Land of Milk and Money*. Their staff worked with us along the way, helping to guide and refine the stories and information included in the book.

Rural Action is a regional community development organization with a 26-county footprint working with members, partners, and community leaders on a range of quality of life, environmental, and economic projects across Appalachian Ohio. Their mission is to build a more just economy by developing the region's assets in socially, financially, and environmentally sustainable ways.

Their vision for Appalachian Ohio is a region with clean streams and healthy forests; a place where thriving family farms, meaningful livelihoods and vibrant communities exist for everyone, with people engaged as good stewards of the world they live in and working together to make this vision a reality.

Rural Action views the people living and working in Appalachian Ohio to be the region's greatest asset. They believe in lifting up local people whose knowledge can be shared with others through peer to peer interactions. Leaders such as Abbe and Madeline as well as the other women owned businesses highlighted in this book, are helping to forge a path for current and future generations of farmers in our region. This book embodies Rural Action's philosophy of peer-led and place-based education.

Building upon that, Rural Action works to give farmers and food businesses the resources they need to share projects and new models they have created to continue building the local food sector as an economic driver in the region.

Rural Action would also like to thank Abbe and Madeline Turner for leading the creation of this valuable toolkit for all specialty dairy producers while highlighting the powerful stories of Ohio women farmers and business owners. Additionally, special thanks to USDA Sustainable Agriculture Research and Education (SARE) - without their support this book would not be possible.

ABOUT ABBE TURNER

Lucky Penny Farm | Garrettsville, OH

Abbe Turner of Lucky Penny Farm inspires women in agriculture (and in any realm) to take the entrepreneurial leap from dreaming to daring-do.

Because there are no shortcuts to success, Abbe says that an agricultural lifestyle is best suited for those with a healthy sense of humor, grit, determination, innovation, motivation and inspiration. You need a song in your heart and a spring in your step, because, without hope and optimism, it's easier to give up than to push forward and pivot as needed.

Success comes to those who learn to diversify, ensuring multiple streams of income. A love for the land and all the good it can provide motivates Abbe to extend her entrepreneurial energies in multiple directions. A flexible stance allows her to pivot her focus and reprioritize resources toward new initiatives in order to maximize rewards.

Recognized as a leader among women in ag, Abbe doesn't just produce quality goods; she creates social good in agricultural, environmental, culinary and non-profit organizations as a business development and fundraising consultant. Lucky Penny Farm and Creamery were named among the "13 Organizations Making Northeast Ohio Greener" by cleveland.com in April 2018. Abbe also earned the Green Business of the Year award in 2014 from the Portage Parks Foundation, became a Farm Aid Farmer Hero in 2013, and was awarded the Kent Chamber of Commerce IMMY Award for significant entrepreneurial investment in 2011. She is also the co-founder of the Ohio Sheep Milk and Cheese Initiative and a member of the OEFFA board of directors.

Ever the collaborator, Abbe has partnered with a number of fellow farmers, cheesemakers, craftspeople, business people and startups in order to mentor them, learn from them, support them, or otherwise magnify their desired outcomes. Abbe's motivation to help others succeed is rooted in her personal story of experimentation, struggle and overcoming roadblocks.

Maybe her risks and rewards are not for everyone, but they are the notes to her life's melody. Abbe agrees with Billie Holiday's sentiments: "If I'm going to sing like someone else, then I don't need to sing at all."

Abbe's still singing her own song.

Please send all correspondence to:

info@artisandairy.com
luckypennycreamery@gmail.com

or

P.O. Box 983
Kent, Ohio 44240

To schedule Abbe Turner and/or Madeline Turner for a motivational speaking engagement, contact Estelle at Sky High Publicity (estelle.ro.bro@gmail.com or 330- 235-3281).

For project management, consulting and design services from farmstead to industrial applications please contact us at info@artisandairy.com or www.artisandairy.com.

ABOUT MADELINE TURNER

One could say that the apple doesn't fall far from the tree. As the eldest child of Abbe Turner, Madeline shares many of the same passions, talents and skills as her mother — pursuing a path of high ambitions, deep purpose and meaningful outcomes all her own, she seeks to contribute to the creation of a more sustainable and just food system through storytelling.

Currently a student at Smith College, Madeline has been recognized for her promise as an entrepreneur and her strength as a leader in response to her skills in public speaking, writing, education, event planning, fundraising and entrepreneurship. She is studying anthropology, ecology, the Middle East and the food system, expecting to earn her bachelor's degree in May 2021.

Coupled with her collegiate studies, Madeline also works as a farmer and food justice educator at both Abundance Farm and Grow Food Northampton in Northampton, Massachusetts. She develops curriculum, leads discussions on food justice with youth, and works with community members to redistribute produce in addition to growing and harvesting food.

Madeline's commitment to sustainability pairs well with her natural talents and learned skills in the multifaceted realm of communications. Her assets come together here, in her first book project, as co-author with her mother Abbe. The apple and the tree work seamlessly together in support of fellow women in agriculture and for the greater good.

ABOUT ESTELLE RODIS-BROWN

Estelle Rodis-Brown is a freelance writer, photographer and public relations/communications specialist working under the business name, Sky High Publicity. Her writing appears in several regional publications, including Northeast Ohio Boomer & Beyond magazine, The Weekly Villager newspaper and Kent State University-Geauga PR. She has also represented Abbe Turner since helping her launch Lucky Penny as a value-added enterprise through a successful USDA grant in 2008. A steady flow of press releases, web content and other marketing material has followed. This is their first shared book project. They are still friends!

Photo Credit: Terry Tung

ABOUT AMBER SATTELBERG

Amber is an aspiring entrepreneur who moonlights (daylights?) as a bookkeeper, gardener, and fiber artist. She strengthened her love of sustainable agriculture during the three years she spent as a Peace Corps Volunteer in Paraguay. Amber currently calls Hudson, Ohio home where she lives with two scrappy dogs and an even scrappier cat.

APPENDIX

I. WOMEN IN DAIRY CONTACT LIST

Marchant Manor
Kandice Marchant
kmmarchak@gmail.com
www.marchantmanor.com

Ferrum Moraine Farm
Gwenn Volkert
gvolkert@me.com
330-221-4581
www.ferrummoraine.com

Hershey Montessori School
Rachel Mckinney
rachelmckinney@windstream.net
440-636-6290
www.hershey-montessori.org

Ayars Family Farm
Bonnie Ayars
ayarsfamilyfarm@gmail.com
937-284-1358
www.ayarsfamilyfarm.com

Old Forge Dairy
Rebecca Oravets
oldforgedairy@gmail.com
330-221-3332
www.oldforgedairy.com

Integration Acres
Michelle Gorman
info@integrationacres.com
740-698-6060
www.integrationacres.com

Pierre's French Ice Cream Co.
Shelly Roth
icecream@pierres.com
216-432-1144
www.pierres.com

Jedidiah Farm
Sarah Taylor
sarah@jedidiahfarm.com
614-625-3461
www.jedidiahfarm.com

Blue Jacket Dairy
Angel King
angel@bluejacketdairy.com
937-292-7327
www.bluejacketdairy.com

Canal Junction Farmstead Cheese
Shiela Schlatter
info@canaljunctioncheese.com
419-393-2799
www.canaljunctioncheese.com

Velvet Ice Cream
Laconda Dager
ldager@velveticecream.com
800-589-5000
www.velveticecream.com

Lucky Penny Creamery
Abbe Turner
abbe@luckypennyfarm.com
330-715-4140
www.luckypennyfarm.com

Lamp Post Cheese
Cecilia Garmendia
cecilia@lamppostcheese.com
513-934-7376
www.lamppostcheese.com

Black Locust
Sasha Sigetic
stargate111@me.com
740-591-5851
www.facebook.com/
blacklocustlivestockandherbal

Clover Road Creamery
Rachel and Sarah Gross
info@cloverroadcreamcheese.com
216-331-2897
www.cloverroadcreamcheese.com

Hastings Dairy
Brenda Hastings
hastings97@gmail.com
440-635-0313
www.hastingsdairy.com

II. RESOURCES

American Dairy Association- Mideast
Tracy Enslen
www.drink-milk.com
614-890-1800
tracy.enslen@drink-milk.com

American Dairy Goat Association
www.adga.com
828-286-3801

American Dairy Science Association
www.adsa.org

Attra Sustainable Agriculture
www.attra.ncat.org
800-346-9140
askanag@ncat.org

Cheez-sorce
Neville McNaughton
www.cheezsorce.com

ChemServe Inc.
www.chemserveinc.com
330-837-7631
office@chemservewest.com

Dairy Foods Consulting
Peter Dixon
www.dairyfoodsconsulting.com
westminsterartisan@gmail.com

Holistic Management International
www.holisticmanagement.org
505-842-5252

NLPA Sheep and Goat Fund
800-237-7193 ext. 10

**NOFA Massachusetts Organic
Dairy Program**
www.nofomass.org/programs/rawmilk/index.php
978-355-2853

NOFA New Work Organic Dairy
www.nofany.org/certification/dairysources.htm

**Northeast Organic Dairy
Producers Alliance**
www.organicmilk.org
413-772-0444

Ohio Dairy Industry Resources Center
www.dairy.osu.edu
614-688-3059
eastridge.1@osu.edu

Ohio Dairy Producer's Association
www.odpa.org

**Ohio Department of Agriculture:
Dairy Division**
www.agri.ohio.gov/wps/portal/gov/oda/
divisions/dairy/home

Ohio Sheep Improvement Association
Roger High
www.ohiosheep.org
614-246-8299

**Organic Livestock and
Grazing Resources**
L. McCrory
www.media.cce.cornell.edu/hosts/
agfoodcommunity/orglivgrazres.pdf
802-434-4122

Rural Action
Tom Redfern
740-677-4047
tomr@ruralaction.org
www.ruralaction.org

SCORE
www.score.org

Small Business Association
www.sba.gov

The American Cheese Society
www.cheesesociety.org
262-728-4458

**The Midwest Organic and Sustainable
Education Services**
www.mosesorganic.org
715-772-3153

USDA
www.usda.gov

Women Grow Ohio
www.ruralaction.org/programs/agriculture

Fertrell Company Blog
Jeff Pennay
https://www.fertrell.com/blog/tag/dairy

Holmes Laboratory
www.holmeslab.com
330.893.2933

Organic Livestock Feed Suppliers Database
attra.ncat.org/attra-pub/livestockfeed_srch.php

Supplemental Dietary Protein for Grazing Dairy Cows: Effect on Pasture Intake and Lactation Performance
www.jds.fass.org/cgi/reprint/84/4/896

The Merck Veterinary Manual
merckvetmanual.com

Dairy Farm Practices Council
www.dairypc.org
732-203-1947

Midwest Plan Service
www.public.iastate.edu/~mwps_dis/mwps_web/frame_p.html

Canada Plan service
www.cps.gov.on.ca

Washington Association of Shareholder Dairy Owners
www.shareholderdairies.org
509-725-0610

University of Wisconsin Center for Cooperatives
www.uwcc.wisc.edu/index.html
608-262-3981

The Center for Dairy Profitability
www.cdp.wisc.edu
608-263-5665

Nat Bacon's Sample Transitioning Budget
www.organicmilk.org/links.html

EnSave
www.ensave.com
800-732-1399

The Wisconsin Public Service Corporation
www.wisconsinpublicservice.com/farm/farm.asp
877-444-0888

Wisconsin Focus on Energy
www.focusonenergy.com
800-762-7077

Strategies for Energy Use on the Dairy Farm
www.traill.uiuc.edu/dairynet/paperDisplay.cfm?COntentID=331

US Dairy Forage Research Center
www.ars.usda.gov/midwest-area/madison-wi/us-dairy-forage-research-center/
608-890-0050

USDA Current Research Information System
www.cris.csrees.usda.gov

SARE Project Reports
www.sare.org/reportungreport_viewer.asp

AGRICOLA From the National Agriculture Library
agricola.nal.usda.gov

State Cooperative Extension and Land-Grant Universities
csrees.esda.gov/qlinks/partners/state_partners.html

ACEnet
Leslie Schaller
https://acenetworks.org/acenet-consulting/toolkits
740-592-3854 ext. 115
LeslieS@acenetworks.org

Kersia
Janice Deuble
www.kersia-group.com
541-667-7502
Janice.deuble@kersia-group.com

FDA Labeling requirements for foodstuffs
https://www.fda.gov/downloads/Food/GuidanceRegulation/

Lucky Penny Kickstarter Video
www.kickstarter.com/projects/771470932/lucky-penny-candy-goats-milk-caramel-cajeta

III. READING LISTS

WOMEN IN ENTREPRENEURSHIP

The Farmstead Creamery Advisor Gianaclis Caldwell
This is the Bible for your business and one of the most important texts you have to read — buy two copies, one to take notes in and one to keep clean.

Tribes: We Need You To Lead Us
Seth Godin
Because leadership is for you.

Growing A Business
Paul Hawken
Sweet book

Frog and Toad Are Friends
Arnold Lobel
Practice making a list, surround yourself with good friends who stick around even on your bad days

The Lean Startup
Eric Ries
A classic, easy to read, relatable

Venture Deals
Brad Feld
Nitty-gritty of funding mechanisms

Disciplined Entrepreneurship
Bill Aulet
A great alternative to the Lean Startup methodology that has many actionable items for potential entrepreneurs.

Charlotte's Web
E.B. White
Helpful for remembering how to dream and think through stories.

The Start-Up Checklist
David S. Rose
Great actionable list for early entrepreneurs to feel like they are progressing while building their business

Mindfulness: A Practical Guide
Tessa Watt
Take more deep breaths.

Dare to Lead
Brene Brown
Reminding us why we have a responsibility to lead, willingness to dare

Business Model Generation + Value Proposition Design
Alex Osterwilder
Creator of the Business Model Canvas, great resource tools for entrepreneurs at any level. A good fit for discovering and iterating the business model and honing the value creation process.

The Art of the Start
Guy Kawasaki
We love this book for its simple style and smart information

Art of the Common Place
Wendell Berry
Thoughts on how we relate to land and each other

David and Goliath
Malcolm Gladwell
An age-old lesson illustrating why leaning on false assumptions is self-defeating

The Alchemist
Paulo Coehlo
Because we are all on a journey.

The Big Enough Company: Creating a Business That Works For You
Adelaide Lancaster and Amy Abrams
Know when to say no

The Art of War
Sun Tzu
Insight into effective strategy

Building a Great Business and The Power of Beliefs in Business
Ari Weinzweig
A lapsed anarchist's approach

Setting the Table
Danny Meyer
Hospitality, humor, and staying humble

Inquiring into the Nature of Slow Money: Investing as if Food, Farms, and Fertility Mattered
Woody Tasch
Slow money is the future

Start With Why
Simon Sinek
Meaningful, inspired leadership is key

Ecopreneuring: Putting Purpose and the Planet Before Profit
John Ivanko & Lisa Kivirist
Sustainability & Business

From Kitchen to Market: Selling Your Gourmet Food Specialty
Stephen F. Hall
Basic, helpful information on starting a food based business

Homemade for Sale: How To Set Up and Market a Food Business From Your Home Kitchen
Lisa Kivirist & John D. Ivanko
Nice profiles on small home-based businesses

AGRICULTURE

CATTLE

The Cattle Health Handbook
Heather Smith Thomas

Essential Guide to Calving
Heather Smith Thomas

An Illustrated Guide to Cows
Celia Lewis

How to Raise Cattle
Philip Hasheider

The Complete Guide to Grass-Fed Cattle
Jacob Bennett

Dairy Herd Health
Martin Green

Dairy Processing and Quality Assurance
Ramesh Chandan

Livestock Handling and Transport
Temple Grandin

Mastitis Control in Dairy Herds
Hendrik Hodeveen
Rebhun's Diseases of Dairy Cattle Thomas Divers

Dairy Cattle Science
Howard Tyler

The Veterinary Book for Dairy Farmers Roger Blowit

Udder Health
Theo Hulsen

CHEESE

Cheesemonger
Edgar Gordon

American Farmstead Cheese
Paul Kinderstedt

Making Artisan Cheese
Tim Smith

The Small-Scale Dairy
Gianaclis Caldwell

Successful Cheesemaking
Merryl Winstein

The Cheese Chronicles
Liz Thorpe

The Cheese Bible
Christian Teubner

The Small-Scale Cheese Business Gianaclis Caldwell

The Cheesemaker's Manual
Margaret Morris

The Cheesemaker's Apprentice
Sasha Davies

Mastering Artisan Cheesemaking Gianaclis Caldwell

200 Easy Homemade Cheese Recipes Debra Amrein-Boyes

Artisan Cheese Making at Home
Mary Darlin

Culture magazine

COOPERATIVES

Cooperatives in the Dairy Industry
USDA Rural

DAIRY COW HEALTH

*Alternative Treatments for Ruminant Animals:
Safe, Natural Veterinary Care for Cattle,
Sheep and Goats*
Paul Dettloff

*Treating Dairy Cows Naturally: Thoughts and
Strategies*
Harold Karreman

Treating Mastitis without Antibiotics
J. Duval

*The Complete Herbal Handbook for Farm and
Stable*
Levy Bairacli

The Herdsman's Introduction to Homeopathy
P. Hansford

ENERGY MANAGEMENT

*Utilization of Renewable Energy Sources and
Energy-Saving Technologies by Small-Scale
Milk Plants and Collection Centres*
G. Riva

FINANCIAL MANAGEMENT

*Building a Sustainable Business: A Guide to
Developing a Business Plan for Farms and
Rural Businesses*
G. DiGiacomo

*Primer for Selecting New Enterprises for Your
Farm*
T. Woods

*The Economics of Organic and Grazing Dairy
Farms*
T. Kriegl

*Dairy Farmer Profitability Using Intensive
Rotational Stocking: Better Grazing
Management for Pastures*
USDA

FOOD SCIENCE

On Food and Cooking
Harold McGee

FORAGES & GRAZING

Grazing Systems Planning Guide
K. Blanchey

*Pasture for Dairy Cattle: Challenges and
Opportunities*
D.M. Amaral-Phillips

Grass for Dairy Cattle
J.H. Cherney

Forage-Animal Management Systems
R. Blaser

*Making the Switch: Two Successful Dairy
Graziers Tell Their Stories*
R. Holter

Management-Intensive Grazing
J. Gerrish

*Pastures for Profit: A Guide to Rotational
Grazing*
D. Undersander

*Prescribed Grazing and Feeding
Management for Lactating Dairy Cows*
D. Emmick

GOATS

Storey's Guide to Raising Dairy Goats
Jerry Belanger

Dairy Goats for Pleasure and Profit
Harvey Considine

How to Raise Goats
Carol Amundsen

Dairy Goats Feeding and Nutrition
Antonello Cannas

The Dairy Goat Handbook
Ann Starbard

How to Raise Dairy Goats
Martha Maeda

Modern Dairy Goats
Mary Gordon

The Dairy Goat Handbook
Ann Starbard

ICE CREAM

The Science of Ice Cream
Chris Clarke

Frozen Desserts
Caroline Liddell

Making Ice Cream and Frozen Yogurt
Maddie Oster

Hello, My Name is Ice Cream
Dana Cree

A to Z Ice Cream
Lisa Bond

The Ultimate Ice Cream Book
Bruce Weinstein

MANAGEMENT

Organic Dairy Farming
Jody Padgham

Dairy Your Way
Meg Moynihan

Milk and Meat from Grass
J.M. Wilkinson

Holistic Management: A New Framework for Decision Making
A. Savory

MARKETING

A Study of Marketing Issues with Organic Milk
R. Hammarlund

NUTRITION

The Mineral Requirements of Grazing Ruminants
N.D. Grace

SHEEP

Storey's Guide to Raising Sheep
Paula Simmons
Sheep
Sue Weaver

The Sheep Book
Ronald Parker

Living with Sheep
Chuck Wooster

The Veterinary Book for Sheep Farmers
David Henderson

Sheep for Beginners
Nigel Woodrup

Natural Sheep Care
Pat Coleby

How to Raise Sheep
Philip Hasheider

Guide to Raising Dairy Sheep
Yves Burger

Principles of Sheep Dairying in North America
Yves Burger

Dairy Sheep Basics for Beginners
David L. Thomas

VALUE-ADDED

Value-Added Dairy Processing Feasibility Report
R. Hammarlund

Questions You Should Answer Before Starting a New Dairy Processing Enterprise
B. Henehan

IV. VENDORS

Agriservice LLC
www.agri-service.com
800-260-3599
Farm equipment

Artisan Dairy
www.artisandairy.com
info@artisandairy.com
(330)715-4140
Agricultural Project Management Fundraising to Facility Design

The Airloom Company
www.theairloomcompany.com/art-craft
Marketing/design/consulting

Brenmar Co.
www.brenmarco.com
865-458-8860
Packaging materials

Caprine Supply
www.caprinesupply.com
800-646-7736
Everything goat!

Central/Valley/Central Valley Dairy Supply
www.dairyandfarmsupply.com
308-380-7188
Animal handling equipment

Chemserve Inc.
www.chemserveinc.com
740-545-6261
Sanitation supplies/consulting

CHR Hansen
www.chr-hansen.com
800-543-4422
Specialty cheese making supplies and enzymes

D-S Livestock Equipment
www.dslivestock.biz
800-949-9997
Livestock handling equipment

Dairy Connection Inc.
www.dairyconnection.com
608-242-9030
Dairy supplies for commercial producers

Flavor seal
www.cmsflavorseal.com
440-937-3900
Packaging material

Fleet Farm
www.fleetfarm.com
877-633-7456
Milking equipment sanitation/vaccines/feed/ farm equipment

Fromagex
www.fromagex.com
866-437-6624
Artisenal and industrial cheese making supplies and equipment

Get Culture
www.getculture.com
608-268-0462
Molds, recipies, books and wax coatings

Glengarry Cheesemaking and Dairy Supplies
www.glengarrycheesemaking.on.ca
613-525-3133
Dairy supplies

Goodwinol Products Corporation
www.goodwinol.com
800-554-1080
Basic medication for sheep and goats

Hamby Dairy Supply
www.hambydairysupply.com
816-449-1314
Feeding supplies/milking equipment/milk processing and transport equipment

Hoegger Supply Company
www.hoeggerfarmyard.com
(770) 703-3072
Goat rearing and cheese making supplies

International Machinery Exchange (IME)
www.imexchange.com
608-764-5481
New and used dairy, cheese, and food machinery

Kelley Supply Inc.
www.kelleysupply.com
800-782-8573
Packaging/sanitation supplies

MicroDairy Designs
www.microdairydesigns.com
301-824-3689
Equipment for small dairies

Nelson Jameson
www.nelsonjameson.com
800-826-8302
Food safety, sanitation and packaging

New England Cheese Making Supply Co.
www.cheesemaking.com
413-397-2012
Cheese making equipment and cultures

Parts Dept
www.partsdeptonline.com
800-245-8222
Dairy equipment and supplies

PBS Animal Health
www.pbsanimalhealth.com
800-321-0235
Sheep, goat, dairy health supplies

Planet Label
www.planetlabel.com
1-866-252-1520
Custom label printing

Premiere Fencing Supply
www.premier1supplies.com/c/fencing
800-282-6631
Fencing

Professional Welding Services
Andrew Ziobert
330-881-8787
Welding services

Rural King
www.ruralking.com
800-561-1762
Fencing/general farm equipment

Sand Creek Post and Beams
www.sandcreekpostandbeam.com
888-489-1680
Farm structures

Standout Stickers
www.standoutstickers.com
330-721-1300
15% off! Promo code "milk"

Sydell
www.sydell.com
605-624-4583
Sheep and goat equipment

The Beverage People
www.thebeveragepeople.com
800-544-1867
Tools, ingredients and small-scale cheese making kits

The Cheese Maker
www.thecheesemaker.com
414-745-5483
Cheese and yogurt making supplies

The Coburn Company Inc.
www.coburn.com
800-776-7042
Goat and sheep milking equipment

Tractor Supply Co.
www.tractorsupply.com
General farm supplies

Ullmer's Dairy Equipment
www.ullmers.com
920-822-8266
Dairy equipment

USA Label Express
www.usalabelexpress.com
330-327-3668
Label printing

Fertrell
www.fertrell.com
(717) 367-1566
Animal Nutrition

Tumbling B's Cattle Co
www.tumblingbcattleco.com
740-503-3120
Artificial insemination for small farmers

Holmes Laboratory
www.holmeslab.com
330.893.2933
Soil, feed and water testing

Berlin Packaging
www.berlinpackaging.com
330-363-9822
Packaging materials

V. LUCKY PENNY CONSTRUCTION COST SHEET

CONSTRUCTION COST PROPOSAL

SOFT COST		TOTAL $2,500.00
Building Permit	$1,100.00	
Dumpster	$1,000.00	
Port-a-potty	$400.00	
Misc		

GENERAL TRADE WORK		TOTAL $36,415.00
Doors/Frames/Hardware	$10,640.00	
Masonry/Demolition/Glazing	$2,800.00	
Demolition/Framing/Signage	$11,375.00	
Project Management	$11,600.00	

MEP WORK		TOTAL $68,471.00
Plumbing/Milk Vat Work	$23,683.00	
HVAC/Mechanical Piping	$23,988.00	
Electrical	$20,800.00	

MISCELLANEOUS		TOTAL $3,800.00
Painting Materials	$2,500.00	
Toilet Accessories	$500.00	
3 Compartment Sink	$800.00	

	RUNNING TOTAL	$111,186.00
CONTINGENCY	7%	$7,783.02
TOTAL PROJECT COST		$118,969.02

VI. LUCKY PENNY TOTAL COST SHEET

Building and Construction (Mechanical/Electric/Plumbing)	$118,000
Pasteurizer/Chart Recorder	$11,000
Air Space Heater	$1,500
Bulk Tank	$2,000
Hoses/Clamps/Gaskets	$1,800
Pumps (3)	$4,500
Motors	$800
Shed for Raw Milk	$1,500
Small Bulk Tank	$1,000
Stainless Steel Tables/Sinks	$3,000
Vacuum Packaging Machine	$5,000
Laundry Washer/Dryer	$1,000
Scale	$400
Refrigerator	$600
Cheese Knives	$1,000
Cheese Molds	$1,600
Milk Cans (12 X $180)	$2,160
Heat Exchanger	$1,000
Boiler	$1,500
Hot Water	$700
Drain Table	$700
Cheese Bags	$500
Walk-In Cooler	$4,000
Brine Tank	$600
Chiller	$1,400
Kettle	$900
Farmers Market Supplies	$1,200
Design and Printing Start Up	$800
Delivery Vehicle/Van	$2,500
Dairy/Cheese Consultants	$3,200
Legal	$3,000
Licensing	$700
Education	$2,500
Building	$86,000

TOTAL	$268,060

Disclaimer: Some things purchased new or used based on availability—Your project will vary.

VII. ODA LICENSING REQUIREMENTS FOR PRODUCERS

The following items must be completed prior to the first shipment of milk from a facility:

1. Completed and signed producer license/registration application;
2. $15 application fee (Check made payable to "Treasurer, State of Ohio");
3. Acceptable water sample from an EPA Certified Lab (<1 for total coliform and <1 for e-coli);
4. Plan submittal form filled out completely, with drawings of your facility showing the location of the milkhouse and milking area, and the items within each area (to include milk flow);
5. Acceptable inspection from the District Sanitarian for your area. Items considered during an inspection are:
   1. Abnormal milking methods and procedures;
   2. Milking area construction, to include floors, walls, ceilings, lighting and ventilation;
   3. Milking area cleanliness;
   4. Cowyard/housing area cleanliness and manure storage;
   5. Milkhouse construction, to include floor, walls and ceiling, and lighting and ventilation;
   6. Milkhouse miscellaneous requirements (size and use, openings, hoseport, etc.);
   7. Milkhouse cleaning facilities (washvats, water heating, water pressure);
   8. Milkhouse cleanliness;
   9. Toilet construction and maintenance (if applicable);
   10. Water supply (type, location, submerged inlets, backflow protection, etc.);
   11. Equipment construction;
   12. Equipment cleaning and sanitizing;
   13. Equipment storage;
   14. Cow cleanliness;
   15. Milk and equipment protection;
   16. Drug and chemical control;
   17. Hand-washing facilities;
   18. Personnel cleanliness;
   19. Milk cooling;
   20. Pest control in and around the facility.

PROPOSED GRADE A FARM
- Application and $15 License Fee
- Plan Submittal Form
- Acceptable Water Sample
- Facility Inspection

NAME CHANGE ON GRADE A FARM
- Application and $15 License Fee
- Plan Submittal Form
- Acceptable Water Sample
- Facility Inspection

PROPOSED MANUFACTURED FARM - CAN MILK
- Application and $15 License Fee
- Acceptable Water Sample
- Facility Inspection

PROPOSED MANUFACTURED FARM - BULK MILK
- Application and $15 License Fee
- Plan Submittal Form
- Acceptable Water Sample
- Facility Inspection

NAME CHANGE ON MANUFACTURE GRADE FARM
- Application and $15 License Fee
- Acceptable Water Sample
- Facility Inspection

MANUFACTURE GRADE - CHANGE FROM CANS TO BULK
- Application and $15 License Fee
- Plan Submittal Form
- Acceptable Water Sample
- Facility Inspection

UPGRADE FROM MANUFACTURE TO GRADE A
- Application and $15 License Fee
- Plan Submittal Form
- Acceptable Water Sample
- Facility Inspection

All above criteria must be met prior to a producer shipping milk

Water sample required in the above criteria shall be taken by the marketing organization

Any farm that has been out of business for more than six months will need to apply as a new farm

VIII. ODA LICENSING REQUIREMENTS FOR PROCESSORS

Below are items that all new processors need to consider before obtaining a Dairy Processor License from the Ohio Department of Agriculture.

1. Building and equipment plans (preparation and submittal)
2. Products to be processed
3. Application and submittal process (including categories to be applied for)
4. Other licenses that may be needed from the Ohio Department of Agriculture. These could include a Milk Hauler License, Weigher, Sampler and Tester License, Milk Producer License and/or a Milk Dealer License.
5. IMS program participation and ramifications
6. Product labeling
7. Drug residue testing and reporting
8. Fee structure and monthly usage reporting
9. Inspection procedures and policies
10. Equipment testing procedures and policies
11. Product sampling requirements
12. Other agency requirements and relationships (EPA, Local Building Codes, FDA, USDA)
13. Questions from you, the prospective processor

IX. SAMPLE MILK RECEIVING CONTRACT

Sample Milk Purchase Rules

All producers must maintain Manufacture Grade while following Grade A practices put forth by the IMS requirements regardless of the market unless noted in the contract. By exception only.

- CFU/US | Raw count less than 100,000
- Somatic Cell | Less than 10 (1 mil)
- PI | Less than 100,000
- Antibiotic | Zero Tolerance

Purchase

We will make every effort to provide a stable market for the purchase of quality milk, but cannot guarantee long term market availability. Milk price is a predetermined cost minus the cost of hauling.

Quality Enforcement

- Antibiotic Residue | No Pay
- Grade A Market: CLU over 200,000 | No Pay
- Raw Count CFU at or over 100,000 | Fined $50 + .05/lb deduction if milk is comingled and next pick up, sample only until issue is addressed and fixed
- Manufacturing Grade | All milk must meet Grade A requirements
- Hydrogen Peroxide, Water adulteration or other species' milk contamination | No Pay
- The Processor will Pay for the regular milk testing unless an issue arises, then the producer will be charged for the cost of additional tests.

Persistent Problems

The buyer reserves the right to terminate the relationship with the producer if an issue/s is/are not resolved in 3 batches or if 3 separate issues appear within 12 months of the first offense.

NOTE:

Counts used are from [name of lab you will be using here]

Any problem found to cause load counts over existing quality allowances will be fined according to damages caused including loss of complete load plus shipping and testing fees as well as processing cost if applicable.

Trucking Fees
- $1.50 per loaded mile
- Trucking costs will be reevaluated at the beginning of each pick up year and based upon current cost and expenses.
- Producer may be assessed additional fees necessary to cover pickup

NOTE: Producer must supply their own state-approved milk cans including a duplicate set for pick up/ drop off exchange.

Milk temperature should not exceed 34°F nor should a block of ice be attached to the bottom of the tank preventing proper cooling on top. Agitating often is recommended (once every half hour) and an adjustable thermometer designated for milk use only should be kept on the premise and calibrated weekly.

Cleaning Procedures

Rinse tanks with warm (never hot) water.

Wash with hot water and chlorine soap. Water temperature should reach 160°F at the beginning of cleaning and should reach no lower than 140°F by the end.

Rinse with an acid rinse.

Sanitize with pasteurized acid, not bleach

Bulk Tank and Milker cleaning instructions:

Do not rinse tank with milk in it- wait until transfer hose is disconnected form tank before rinsing. High PI counts are often a result of water contamination. When cleaning, make sure the underside of the lid, agitator, and entire outlet area (inside and out) are cleaned. Disassemble valve when cleaning. Vacuum line should be cleaned daily with hot water. Make sure to drain on low end of vacuum line to prevent water retention. For bucket milkers, make sure the flexible hose to the bucket lid has a loop to prevent condensation contamination or milk overflow into vacuum line. Clear hoses are a good investment as they are easier to monitor.

Price/CWT: _____ **Date:** _____

Producer: _____

Purchaser: _____

X. HACCP - SAFETY FIRST

Amber Sattelberg

Adopt a HACCP Plan to Prevent Food Safety Mishaps

The keystone of any food production or processing operation is safety. Before profit, before quality, before scale, a food-based business must ensure that it is providing the public with a product that is safe to eat. At the very best in the aftermath of a food-borne illness scandal, the company in question will suffer massive economic loss. At the very worst, lives of consumers could be at stake. Realizing the importance of providing consumers with sanitary nourishment, several food corporations along with NASA developed the Hazard Analysis Critical Control Point (HACCP) system in order to prevent food safety mishaps that would jeopardize the companies or customers in question. A HACCP plan breaks down the steps that go into handling the food product before it reaches the consumer and identifies crucial points in the process where things could go wrong.

As one might expect (being that NASA was involved in the establishment of this standard assessment process), HACCP plans can be somewhat time-consuming and involved to write up. No, it isn't rocket science, but it does beg careful examination of the operating plans and procedures that are followed within the facility. As a precursor to a HAACP plan, any production or processing facility that handles food should have a Prerequisite Program to establish standard operating procedure that will, in and of itself, reduce the risk of contamination of food. The Prerequisite Program is part of the HACCP system but differs from the HACCP Plan in that the Program outlines the general functioning of the entire plant, from infrastructure to personal hygiene and everything between. In contrast, a HACCP Plan focuses on very specific Critical Control Points where potential for the introduction of food to hazards is likely to happen despite the best practices outlined in the plan.

The Prerequisite Plan for an operation should first examine the building where manufacturing is taking place, be it a designated factory or an on-farm facility. Guidelines for determining best practices for on-farm milk production can be found online on a variety of sites, and www.dairypc.org, in particular, has a breadth of free downloadable guidelines for implementing and maintaining sanitary practices on the farm. Once the product leaves the milking room, Good Manufacturing Practices (GMPs) will help to ensure that clean milk doesn't become contaminated via improper handling and treatment. These practices typically fall into one of four categories:

1. **Personal Hygiene:** No, this isn't arguing that Fred's decision to forgo deodorant is a food safety hazard. Rather, the personal hygiene aspect of GMPs focuses on policies regarding attire (hair nets, sterile boots, clean nails etc.), health (what's the policy regarding sick employees?), the prohibition of eating or smoking in the facility, policy regarding hand washing (yes, everyone certainly hopes that this doesn't need to be explained to others, but it's always better to be safe than sorry), and policies for visitors to the facility. Maybe policies regarding deodorant usage could be included, too.

2. **Building and Facilities:** There is some overlap here between standards for a milking facility and a processing facility, namely the need for sanitary water, adequate pest management and maintenance of the grounds. In addition, manufacturing facilities require restrooms and handwashing facilities to allow personnel to adhere to the personal hygiene standards outlined in the previous step. There should also be appropriate lighting, ventilation and garbage removal/disposal systems in place.

3. **Equipment and Utensils:** All of the handwashing and clean water in the world will not prevent food contamination if the utensils that come in contact with the product are not appropriate for use in dairy processing or sanitized properly. This set of GMPs should address practices that affect the cleanliness and efficacy of everything that will come in contact with the product.

4. **Production and Process Control:** As with the Personal Hygiene segment of these GMPs, Production and Process Controls indicate actionable steps that are to be taken by personnel within the facility. These can include process-based actions (packaging practices, storage and cleaning/sanitizing processing areas) as well as recordkeeping (time/temperature control charts, purchase and shipping of ingredients, lot ID).

Though many facilities implement GMPs (even if they're not explicitly stated) there are definite advantages to keeping written records of Best Practices. Not only can this written document provide transparency for customers buying products from the plant, but it can also serve as a training tool for new employees. That is, of course, in addition to the benefit it affords in the creation of the HACCP Plan. The more legwork that is done before sitting down to write the HACCP Plan itself, the easier it will be.

As a complement to GMPs, facilities that work with food (especially dairy, where microbes are used in the creation of a product), Sanitation Standard Operating Procedures (SSOPs) should be written and recorded. The SSOP should provide the "How" to the GMP's "Process Control" and "Clean Utensil" requirement. SSOPs typically include step-by-step procedures for cleaning and sanitizing rooms and equipment as well as checklists to keep a record of sanitation procedures that take place daily, weekly, monthly, or a few times a year. In addition, "Sanitation" procedures can elaborate upon broad GMPs (when do employees have to wash their hands, how often are water sources being tested for sanitation, etc.)

Once these Prerequisite Programs are in place, writing out a HACCP plan will be much easier. The prior steps function to minimize the chance that food products will come in contact with contaminants (or "hazards"). However, the best-laid plans of mice and men can't always keep milk safe from its environment. For this reason, HACCP Plans must be thought through carefully.

The first step in creating a HACCP Plan is to define the products that will be coming out of your facility. Once this has been done, a separate HACCP Plan should be written for each product. Upon selection of a product to begin working on, the next step is to draw a flow-chart of the production processes involved in the manufacturing of the good in question. It does not have to be complicated and it doesn't have to be pretty. It simply must help you visualize the steps your food product will go through before leaving your facility.

Production Process Flow Chart

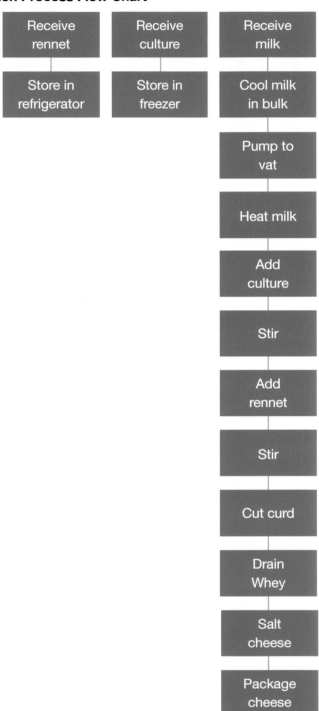

After completing the flow chart, it should be fairly simple to look through the outlined steps to identify what kinds of hazards are presented at each one. Hazards are, simply put, contaminants. They can fall into one of three categories: Chemical (antibiotics, cleaning solution, etc.), Biological (Staph., E. Coli, Listeria, etc.) or Physical (hay, manure, insects). The following is a chart detailing hazards found in the steps outlined in the example above.

PROCESS STEP	HAZARDS
Receive milk	Pathogen, Chemical (antibiotics), Physical (hay, manure)
Cool milk in bulk tank	Pathogen, Chemical (cleaning solution)
Pump milk to vat	Pathogens, Chemical (cleaning solution in pipes/vat)
Heat milk	Pathogens
Add culture	Pathogens, Physical (packaging falling into vat)
Stir	Pathogens
Add rennet	Pathogens (packaging falling into vat)
Stir	Pathogens
Cut curd	Pathogens
Drain whey	Pathogens
Salt cheese	Pathogens
Package cheese	Pathogens

Once hazards have been identified for each step, the table can be expanded to reflect the significance of each of these. Even if it hasn't been determined that a certain category of hazard exists for a specific step, it is still important to document that it has been considered. For example, regardless whether physical hazards (P) are not likely to occur in the cooling of the milk, the table should still include the "P" followed by "None" or "N/A" to reflect the fact that the hazard has been considered and was not simply forgotten.

Process Step	Potential hazard introduced controlled of enhanced	Is the food safety hazard significant?	Justify your decision	What control measures can be applied to prevent significant hazards?
Receive milk	B: Pathogens in milk	Yes	Pathogens may be present in raw milk	Receive milk at proper temperatures (45^{0}F)
	C: antibiotics	No	Suppliers provide test results showing the absence of antibiotics upon delivery	Store milk below 45^{0}F
	P: Hay/ manure	No	SSOPs in place prevent this	
Cool milk in bulk tank	B: Pathogens in milk	Yes	Pathogens may proliferate in milk	
	C: cleaning solution	No	SSOPs in place	
	P: N/A			
Pump milk to vat	B: Pathogens in milk/ pipes	No	SSOPs in Place	
	C: cleaning solution in pipes/ vat	No	SSOPs in Place	
	P: N/A			

Once **significant** hazards in the production process have been identified, follow this decision tree to determine where the critical control points in your operation lie. Keep in mind, these are the hazards that are LIKELY to be factors in the production system and to pose a significant risk to consumers despite the implantation of and adherence to Prerequisite Plans.

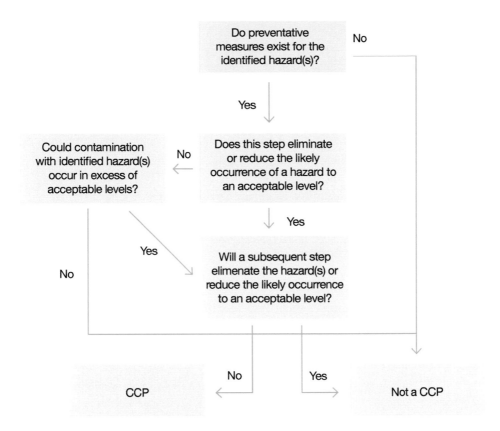

Upon identifying the Critical Control Points within your system, you can now define the critical limits by which you will determine whether corrective actions must be taken to address hazards. In the example outlined above, the only identifiable CCP is the cooling of the milk. While other hazards COULD occur in other steps within the process, those steps do not meet the requirements to qualify as critical control points as per the decision tree provided above. As such, we will focus our efforts on these steps of the cheesemaking process.

Having identified hazards and critical control points, it is now time to determine the critical limits for the steps in question. Critical Limits should be dictated by numbers from reputable sources such as scientific publication, regulatory guidelines (FDA, ODA, USDA) and experts. When setting Critical Limits, it is important to justify why the limit was selected, and where the data behind it came from. In this case, FDA guidelines state that milk must be cooled to 41°F within 2 hours of milking and should be maintained at a temperature no higher than 41°F, so that is justification enough for setting this as a Critical Limit.

All of the work conducted so far would be for naught without a way to translate the study into action. The establishment of Monitoring Procedures for CCPs is the avenue by which this is accomplished. For each CCP, it should be determined how often it will be monitored, who will be responsible for doing so, how it will be recorded that the monitoring took place, and what equipment will be needed in order to assess the Critical Limits set in the previous step. As with everything discussed thus far, it is of utmost importance that these institution-specific regulations be written down. This will help employees, owners and consumers in the long run and will make sure that in the future time isn't wasted reinventing the wheel.

The establishment of Corrective Actions naturally follows the monitoring process. In a perfect world, Critical Limits would never be surpassed and there would be no need for this step, but being that the world is perfectly imperfect, it is more than likely that at some point Corrective Actions will need to be taken in order to address not meeting Critical Limits. The appropriate response to a deviation will be based upon a few crucial questions: Is the product safe? If not, is there some way to make the product safe? Is there a way to perform a test to determine if the product is safe? If the answers to these questions are no's across the board, the product must be thrown away. Failure to adhere to CCPs can be an expensive and time-consuming mistake, as such Corrective Actions also encompass taking steps to analyze what went wrong and what can be done to prevent it from happening in the future. Records should be kept for every incident that requires Corrective Actions, including the affected batch numbers, date, Corrective Actions taken, and how the product was disposed of if there was no way to guarantee its food-safe status.

At this point, the HACCP System and the Plan itself should be fleshed out and ready to put into action. However, as with any structure or framework, a HACCP plan will only serve as well as it is maintained and monitored. As the goal of the HACCP system is to ensure that food products leaving a facility are safe for consumers, the first question one should ask when seeking to Validate and Verify their plan is, "Does this result in a safe food product?" If the answer is no, the entire plan needs to be reexamined. If the answer is yes, it is ready to go into action, for the time being. This question will need to be asked again whenever there is a change in process or product, if frequent problems arise, or if the facility's standard operating procedures are deemed legally unacceptable.

Verifying the efficacy of a HACCP plan is done via several different avenues: calibration of equipment that is used to monitor CCPs, targeted sampling and testing of product, annual HACCP reassessment and revision, and through regulatory agencies. All of these methods should be used to ensure that any HACCP System is working as it was intended. As in all of the previous steps, actions taken to verify and validate the working Plan should be recorded for later review should the need arise.

The development of a HACCP Plan is no small feat, but neither is it of small importance. Food safety practices save lives (and companies) and should be approached with gravity and diligence. Though the budding dairy entrepreneur will, no doubt, have many demands on her time and energy, the development of a written plan to address food safety should be placed near the top of any to-do list. For more information and assistance in developing a food safety plan, producers and processors are encouraged to visit any of the following:

FDA: www.fda.gov
National Food Safety Database: www.foodsafety.org
International Dairy Foods Association: www.idfa.org
National Advisory Committee on Microbiological Criteria for Foods—HACCP Principles and Application Guidelines: www.fst.vt.edu/haccp97
A sample HACCP Program can be found at:
www.cfsan.fda.gov/-comm/haacpdai.html

XI. FDA FARM INSPECTION SHEET

DEPARTMENT OF HEALTH AND HUMAN SERVICES FOOD AND DRUG ADMINISTRATION	**DAIRY FARM INSPECTION REPORT**	INSPECTING AGENCY
NAME AND LOCATION OF DAIRY FARM		POUNDS SOLD DAILY
		PLANT
		PERMIT NO.

Inspection of your dairy farm today showed violations existing in the Items checked below. You are further notified that this inspection report serves as notification of the intent to suspend your permit if the violations noted are not in compliance at the time of the next inspection. (Refer to Sections 3 and 5 of the **Grade "A" Pasteurized Milk Ordinance**.)

XI. FDA FARM INSPECTION SHEET

Continued...

COWS

1. Abnormal Milk:

Cows secreting abnormal milk milked last or in separate equipment..
(a)
Abnormal milk properly handled and disposed of...........................
(b)
Proper care of abnormal milk handling equipment.........................
(c)

MILKING BARN, STABLE, OR PARLOR

2. Construction:

Floors, gutters, and feed troughs of concrete or equally impervious materials; in good repair.....................................
(a)
Walls and ceilings smooth, painted or finished adequately; in good repair; ceiling dust-tight..
(b)
Separate stalls or pens for horses, calves, and bulls; no overcrowding...
(c)
Adequate natural and/or artificial light; well distributed...............
(d)
Properly ventilated...
(e)

3. Cleanliness:

Clean and free of litter...
(a)
No swine or fowl...
(b)

4. Cowyard:

Graded to drain; no pooled water or wastes...............................
(a)
Cowyard clean; cattle housing areas and manure packs properly maintained..
(b)
No Swine...
(c)
Manure stored inaccessible to cows.......................................
(d)

MILKHOUSE OR ROOM

5. Construction and Facilities:

Floors
Smooth; concrete or other impervious material; in good repair.........
(a)
Graded to drain..
(b)
Drains trapped, if connected to sanitary system..........................
(c)

Walls and Ceilings
Approved material and finish...
(a)
Good repair (windows, doors, and hoseport included)......................
(b)

Lighting and Ventilation
Adequate natural and/or artificial light; properly distributed...........
(a)
Adequate ventilation...
(b)
Doors and windows closed during dusty weather............................
(c)
Vents and lighting fixtures properly installed...........................
(d)

Miscellaneous Requirements
Used for milkhouse operations only; sufficient size......................
(a)
No direct opening into living quarters or barn, except as permitted by *Ordinance*...
(b)
Liquid wastes properly disposed of.......................................
(c)
Proper hoseport where required...
(d)
Acceptable surface under hoseport..
(e)
Suitable shelter for transport truck as required.........................

Cleaning Facilities
Two-compartment wash and rinse vat of adequate size......................
(a)
Suitable water heating facilities..
(b)
Water under pressure piped to milkhouse..................................
(c)

6. Cleanliness:
Floors, walls, windows, tables and similar non-product contact surfaces clean..
(a)
No trash, unnecessary articles, animals or fowl..........................
(b)

TOILET AND WATER SUPPLY

7. Toilet:
Provided; conveniently located...
(a)
Constructed and operated according to *Ordinance*.......................
(b)
No evidence of human wastes about premises...............................
(c)
Toilet room in compliance with *Ordinance*..............................
(d)

8. Water Supply:
Constructed and operated according to *Ordinance*.......................
(a)
Complies with bacteriological standards..................................
(b)
No connection between safe and unsafe supplies; no improper submerged inlets...
(c)

UTENSILS AND EQUIPMENT

9. Construction:
Smooth, impervious, nonabsorbent, safe materials; easily cleanable...
(a)
In good repair; accessible for inspection................................
(b)
Approved single-service articles; not reused.............................
(c)
Utensils and equipment of proper design..................................
(d)
Approved mechanically cleaned milk pipeline system.......................
(e)

10. Cleaning:
Utensils and equipment clean...
(a)

11. Sanitization:
All multi-use containers and equipment subjected to approved sanitization process (Refer to *Ordinance*)...........................
(a)

12. Storage:
All multi-use containers and equipment properly stored...................
(a)
Stored to assure complete drainage, where applicable.....................
(b)
Single-service articles properly stored..................................
(c)

MILKING

13. Flanks, Udders, and Teats:
Milking done in barn, stable, or parlor..................................
(a)
Brushing completed before milking begun..................................
(b)
Flanks, bellies, udders, and tails of cows clean at time of milking; clipped when required..
(c)
Teats cleaned, treated with sanitizing solution (if required) and dried, just prior to milking..
(d)
No wet hand milking..
(e)

TRANSFER/PROTECTION OF MILK

14. Protection From Contamination:
No overcrowding..
(a)
Product and mechanical cleaning circuits separated.......................
(b)
Improperly handled milk discarded..
(c)
Immediate removal of milk..
(d)
Milk and equipment properly protected....................................
(e)
Sanitized milk surfaces not exposed to contamination.....................
(f)
Air under pressure of proper quality.....................................
(g)

15. Drug and Chemical Control:
Cleaners and sanitizers properly identified..............................
(a)
Drug administration equipment properly handled and stored................
(b)
Drugs properly labeled (name and address) and stored.....................
(c)
Drugs properly labeled (directions for use, cautionary statements, active ingredient(s))..
(d)
Drugs properly used and stored to preclude contamination of Milk..
(e)

PERSONNEL

16. Handwashing Facilities:
Proper handwashing facilities convenient to milking operations...
(a)
Wash and rinse vats not used as handwashing facilities...................
(b)

17. Personnel Cleanliness:
Hands washed clean and dried before milking, or performing milkhouse functions; rewashed when contaminated.......................
(a)
Clean outer garments worn..
(b)

COOLING

18. Cooling:
Milk cooled to 45°F or less within 2 hours after milking, except as permitted by *Ordinance*......................................
(a)
Recirculated cooling water from safe source and properly protected; complies with bacteriological standards.......................
(b)
An acceptable recording device shall be installed and maintained when required...
(c)

PEST CONTROL

19. Insect and Rodent Control:
Fly breeding minimized by approved manure disposal methods (Refer to *Ordinance*).....................................
(a)
Manure packs properly maintained...
(b)
All milkhouse openings effectively screened or otherwise protected; doors tight and self-closing; screen doors open outward..
(c)
Milkhouse free of insects and rodents....................................
(d)
Approved pesticides; used properly.......................................
(e)
Equipment and utensils not exposed to pesticide contamination..
(f)
Surroundings neat and clean; free of harborages and breeding areas..
(g)
Feed storage not attraction for birds, rodents or insects................
(h)

XI. FDA FARM INSPECTION SHEET

Continued...

REMARKS

DATE	SANITARIAN

Note: Item numbers correspond to required sanitation Items for Grade "A" raw milk for pasteurization in the **Grade "A" Pasteurized Milk Ordinance**

XII. FDA PRODUCTION FACILITY INSPECTION SHEET

Department of Health and Human Services Public Health Service Food and Drug Administration	**MILK PLANT INSPECTION REPORT** (Includes Dry Milk/Condensing Plants, Receiving Stations, Transfer Stations, and Milk Tank Truck Cleaning Facilities)	INSPECTING AGENCY

NAME AND LOCATION OF PLANT	POUNDS SOLD DAILY
	Milk _____
	Other Milk _____
	Products _____
	Total _____
	Permit _____
	No.

Inspection of your plant today showed violations existing in the Items checked below. You are further notified that this inspection report serves as notification of the intent to suspend your permit if the violations noted are not in compliance at the time of the next inspection. (Refer to Sections 3 and 5 of the *Grade "A" Pasteurized Milk Ordinance*.)

XII. FDA PRODUCTION FACILITY INSPECTION SHEET

Continued...

1. FLOORS:
Smooth; impervious; no pools; good repair; trapped drains ....
(a)

2. WALLS AND CEILINGS:
Smooth; washable; light-colored; good repair ....
(a)

3. DOORS AND WINDOWS:
All outer openings effectively protected against entry of
flies and rodents ....
(a)
Outer doors self-closing; screen doors open outward ....
(b)

4. LIGHTING AND VENTILATION:
Adequate light in all rooms ....
(a)
Well ventilated to preclude odors and condensation;
filtered air with pressure systems ....
(b)

5. SEPARATE ROOMS:
Separate rooms as required; adequate size........
(a)
No direct opening to barn or living quarters ....
(b)
Storage tanks properly vented ....
(c)

6. TOILET FACILITIES:
Complies with local Ordinances ....
(a)
No direct opening to processing rooms; self-closing
doors ....
(b)
Clean; well-lighted and ventilated; proper facilities........
(c)
Sewage and other liquid wastes disposed of in sanitary
manner ....
(d)

7. WATER SUPPLY:
Constructed and operated in accordance with Ordinance........
(a)
No direct or indirect connection between safe and unsafe
water ....
(b)
Condensing water and vacuum water in compliance with
Ordinance requirements ....
(c)
Reclaim water complies with Ordinance ....
(d)
Complies with bacteriological standards ....
(e)

8. HAND-WASHING FACILITIES:
Located and equipped as required; clean and in good
repair; improper facilities not used ....
(a)

9. MILK PLANT CLEANLINESS:
Neat; clean; no evidence of insects or rodents; trash
properly handled ....
(a)
No unnecessary equipment ....
(b)
No excessive product dust ....
(c)

10. SANITARY PIPING:
Smooth; impervious; corrosion-resistant; non-toxic; easily
cleanable materials; good repair; accessible for
inspection ....
(a)
Mechanically cleaned lines meet Ordinance specs ....
(b)
Pasteurized products conducted in sanitary piping, except
as permitted by Ordinance ....
(c)

**11. CONSTRUCTION AND REPAIR OF CONTAINERS AND
EQUIPMENT:**
Smooth; impervious; corrosion-resistant; non-toxic; easily
cleanable materials; good repair; accessible for inspection........
(a)
Self-draining; strainers and sifters of approved design ....
(b)
Approved single-service articles; not reused ....
(c)

**12. CLEANING AND SANITIZING OF CONTAINERS/
AND EQUIPMENT:**
Containers, utensils, and equipment effectively cleaned ....
(a)
Mechanical cleaning requirements of Ordinance in
compliance; records complete; milk tank trucks cleaned
at permitted location ....
(b)
Approved sanitization process applied prior to use of
product-contact surfaces ....
(c)

13. STORAGE OF CLEANED CONTAINERS AND EQUIPMENT:
Stored to assure drainage and protected from contamination ....
(a)

14. STORAGE OF SINGLE-SERVICE ARTICLES:
Received, stored and handled in a sanitary manner;
paperboard containers not reused except as permitted
by the Ordinance ....
(a)

15a. PROTECTION FROM CONTAMINATION:
Operations conducted and located so as to preclude
contamination of milk, milk products, ingredients,
containers, equipment, and utensils ....
(a)
Air and steam used to process products in compliance
with Ordinance ....
(b)
Approved pesticides, safely used ....
(c)

15b. CROSS CONNECTIONS:
No direct connections between pasteurized and raw milk or milk
products ....
(a)
Overflow, spilled and leaked products or ingredients
discarded ....
(b)
No direct connections between milk or milk products and
cleaning and/or sanitizing solutions ....
(c)

16a. PASTEURIZATION-BATCH:
(1) INDICATING AND RECORDING THERMOMETERS:
Comply with Ordinance Specifications ....
(a)
(2) TIME AND TEMPERATURE CONTROLS :
Adequate agitation throughout holding; agitator
sufficiently submerged ....
(a)
Each pasteurizer equipped with indicating and recording
thermometer; bulb submerged ....
(b)
Recording thermometer reads no higher than indicating
thermometer ....(c)
Product held minimum pasteurization temperature
continuously for 30 minutes, plus filling time if product
preheated before entering vat, plus emptying time, if
cooling is begun after opening outlet ....
(d)
No product added after holding begun ....
(e)
Airspace above product maintained at not less than 5°F (3°C)
higher than minimum required pasteurization
temperature during holding ....
(f)
Approved airspace thermometer; bulb not less than 1 inch
(25 mm) above product level ....
(g)
Inlet and outlet valves and connections in compliance with
Ordinance ....
(h)

16b. PASTEURIZATION-HIGH TEMPERATURE:
(1) INDICATING AND RECORDING THERMOMETERS:
Comply with Ordinance specifications ....
(a)
(2) TIME AND TEMPERATURE CONTROLS:
Flow-diversion device complies with Ordinance
requirements ....
(a)
Recorder controller complies with Ordinance
requirements ....
(b)
Holding tube complies with Ordinance requirements ....
(c)
Flow promoting devices comply with Ordinance
requirements ....
(d)
Product held minimum pasteurization time and temperature ....
(e)
(3) ADULTERATION CONTROLS: Satisfactory means to
prevent adulteration with added water ....

16c. ASEPTIC PROCESSING SYSTEMS:
(1) INDICATING AND RECORDING THERMOMETERS:
Comply with Ordinance specifications ....
(a)
(2) TIME AND TEMPERATURE CONTROLS:
Flow-diversion device complies with Ordinance
requirements ....
(a)

Recorder controller complies with Ordinance
requirements ....
(b)
Holding tube complies with Ordinance requirements ....
(c)
Flow promoting devices comply with Ordinance
requirements ....
(d)
(3) ADULTERATION CONTROLS:
Satisfactory means to prevent adulteration with added
water ....

16d. REGENERATIVE HEATING:
Pasteurized or aseptic product in regenerator automatically under
greater pressure than raw product in regenerator
at all times ....
(a)
Accurate pressure gauges installed as required; booster
pump properly identified, when required, and installed ....
(b)
Regenerator pressures meet Ordinance requirements ....
(c)

16e. RECORDING CHARTS:
Batch pasteurizer charts comply with applicable Ordinance
requirements ....
(a)
HTST and HHST pasteurizer charts comply with applicable
Ordinance requirements ....
(b)
Aseptic charts comply with applicable Ordinance
requirements ....
(c)

17. COOLING OF MILK AND MILK PRODUCTS:
Raw milk maintained at 45°F (7°C) or less until processed or
as provided for in the Ordinance ....
(a)
Pasteurized milk and milk products, except those to be cultured,
or as provided for in the Ordinance, cooled immediately to 45°F
(7°C) or less in approved equipment; all milk and milk products
stored there until delivered ....
(b)
Approved thermometer properly located in all refrigeration
rooms and storage tanks as required ....
(c)
Recirculated cooling water from a safe source and properly
protected; complies with bacteriological standards ....
(d)

18. BOTTLING, PACKAGING AND CONTAINER FILLING:
Performed in a plant where contents finally pasteurized,
except for dry milk and whey products ....(a)
Performed in a sanitary manner by approved mechanical
equipment ....
(b)
Aseptic filling in compliance ....
(c)
Dry milk and whey products packaged in new containers;
stored and transported in a sanitary manner ....(d)

19. CAPPING, CONTAINER CLOSURE AND SEALING:
Capping and/or closing/sealing performed in a sanitary manner
by approved mechanical equipment ....
(a)
Imperfectly capped/closed products properly handled ....
(b)
Caps and/or closures comply with Ordinance ....
(c)

20. PERSONNEL CLEANLINESS:
Hands thoroughly washed before performing plant functions;
rewashed when contaminated ....
(a)
Clean outer garments and hair covering worn ....
(b)
No use of tobacco in processing areas ....
(c)
Clean boot covers, caps and coveralls worn when
entering dryer ....
(c)

21. VEHICLES:
Vehicles clean; constructed to protect milk ....
(a)
No contaminating substances transported ....
(b)

22. SURROUNDINGS:
Neat and clean; free of pooled water, harborages, and
breeding areas ....
(a)
Tank unloading areas properly constructed ....
(b)
Approved pesticides, used properly ....
(c)

XII. FDA PRODUCTION FACILITY INSPECTION SHEET

Continued...

REMARKS	
DATE	SANITARIAN

1....A receiving station shall comply with Items 1 to 15, inclusive, and 17, 20, and 22. Separation requirements of item 5 do not apply.
2....A transfer station shall comply with Items 1, 4, 6, 7, 8, 9, 10, 11, 12, 13, 14, 15, 20, 22 and as climatic and operating conditions require, applicable provisions of Items 2 and 3. In every case, overhead protection shall be required.
3.... Facilities for the cleaning and sanitizing of milk tank trucks shall comply with the same requirements for transfer stations.

NOTE – Item numbers correspond to required sanitation items for Grade "A" pasteurized milk in the *Grade "A" Pasteurized Milk Ordinance*.

XIII. MARKET KIT LIST

- Apron
- Tablecloth(s)
- Bag for Trash
- Banner
- Bungees or Twine for Banners
- Weights for Tents
- Tent
- Business Cards
- Starter Cash
- Cooler
- Thermometer in Cooler
- Ice Packs
- Sampling Ice
- Sample Cheese/Milk
- Inventory
- Spoons for Sampling
- Spoons for Cheese
- Bowls for Sampling
- Ice Bucket for Milk Sampling
- Milk Sample Cups
- Bowls for Pretzels/Spoons
- Bin for Used Spoons/Cups

- Market Booklet/Rules
- Mobile License
- Paper Towels/Napkins
- Small Paper Bags
- Pictures of Goats
- Sign with Address
- Sales Sign with Prices
- Sales Sheet
- Bins for Sampling
- Disinfectant Wipes
- Sample Sign Holders
- Folding Table(s)
- Gloves
- Hand Sanitizer
- Health Certificate
- Sharpies/Pens/Chalk/Dry Erase
- Soap
- Pretzels
- Mini Bowl for Sample
- Postcards
- Sign
- Loyalty Cards

XIV. MARKET DAY SALES SHEET

Market:	Date:
Weather:	Event:
Name:	Signature:

MARKET DAY SALES SHEET		
	Cash in Bag at Start	Cash in Bag at End
$10.00		
$5.00		
$1.00		
$0.25		
$0.10		
$0.05		
$0.01		
TOTAL		

	Beginning Inventory	Total Sold	Number Returned
Product 1			
Product 2			
Product 3			
Product 4			
Product 5			

Comments:

XV. ACENET DESIGNING YOUR BRAND IDENTITY: LOGOS

BUILDING A BRAND FOR SPECIALTY DAIRY

DESIGNING YOUR BRAND IDENTITY: *LOGOS*

November 7, 2018

Originally, the word "brand" referred to some sort of mark, vessel or covering that indicated that a specific item was the genuine article. A good example is the symbols that silversmiths stamp on the base of silverware. This brand identifies the maker, the year he made the artifact and the city in which it was made. Another common example of "brand" are the unique marks branded onto cattle by ranchers which identify the ranch that owns the cattle.

CREATE A MEMORABLE LOGO

How does this relate to the small business owner? When you create a brand for your company you create a visual image that will stay in people's minds and will be recognized as your company. Your logo is the thing people will associate with your brand and use it to quickly identify your products. Some companies have done this so successfully that they eventually became household names: name such as Band-Aid (who asks for a plastic bandage strip?), Nike, Tylenol, Jeep, and Kleenex.

FIRST IMPRESSIONS

The local food movement is, at the core, bringing a "face" to your food. When shopping in national chain grocery stores, agriculture and farming could be seen as a faceless industry. Consumers do not

have the knowledge and comfort of knowing where and how their food was raised before it goes on the shelves. Your logo will be regarded as the public face of your business and be the initial impression of your brand that people see when they purchase your product.

FACTORS TO CONSIDER

There are several factors to consider when choosing a logo for your business:

• Does your logo match your market segment?
• Is it legible scaled at both a large and small size?
• Does it clearly communicate your brand identity? (place, character, story)
• Will it have longevity and allow for product diversification?
• Is it upgradeable?
• Can it be adjusted to remain current without confusing brand recognition?
• Do your color choices enhance your product?

What do you want your logo to convey to consumers? Your logo should reflect the values you hold when producing your dairy products. For producers in the food sector, it is critical to present yourself as trustworthy. An effective logo will portray a business that your consumers

This Toolkit was supported by the Sustainable Agriculture Research and Education Program.

1

feel they can trust. As you can see in the Creekside Farm logo, it is simple and memorable to consumers, who can recognize the two rolling hills and the flowing creek.

Lucky Penny Creamery owner, Abbe Turner, developed her logo which spans her entire product line, from soaps to the farm. Abbe's logo pays homage to the first dairy goat on her farm.

RECOGNIZABILITY

With over 80% of Americans living in urban areas, local meat producers can take capitalize on the interest in the farming industry by consumers. Popular logos may include imagery like open fields and trees, friendly animals, or farm tools. Using images immediately

helps consumers identify with your brand. Below you will notice the simple sheep on the "Find A Way Farm" logo. This simple picture is immediately recognizable to fans of the brand.

CHOOSING COLORS

With the food production industry so deeply grounded to the planet, earthy tones are common for agricultural producer labels. For example, brown is said to trigger a sense of reliability and support while greens encourage feelings of harmony, refreshment, and peace. Choose colors that you think would appeal to your target customers while conveying your unique features. Choose colors for your logo that are bright and easy to read, even when the image is reduced in size.

NAME IN LOGO

Integrating the name of your business or farm into your logo is an easy and effective way for consumers to connect the company with the visuals they are seeing.

HARMONY

HAPPINESS

RELIABILITY

RELAXATION

This Toolkit was supported by the Sustainable Agriculture Research and Education Program.

SARE
Sustainable Agriculture
Research & Education

ACEnet

Rural Action

2

XVI. ACENET DESIGNING YOUR BRAND IDENTITY: SOCIAL MEDIA

BUILDING A BRAND FOR SPECIALTY DAIRY
AFFORDABLE MARKETING TOOL: *SOCIAL MEDIA*

November 7, 2018

FREE MARKETING & ADVERTISING

Social media can be a cost free method to market your meat products, your farm or your retail business. If you are selling in direct or wholesale markets it is also an extremely effective way to connect directly with customers and buyers. Promoting your brand also gives you endless opportunities to market your partners: retailers, distributors, farm stands, food hubs, and farmers market, to name just a few possible collaborators.

```
Greek Salad | 8   Half | 4.5
The garden salad topped with local feta cheese and kalamata olives.

Caesar Salad | 6   Half | 3.5
Romaine, lettuce, garlic croutons, parmesan cheese & house made caesar vina grette.

Roasted Chicken & Chevre Salad | 10   Half | 5
Ohio produced spring mix, topped with local chicken roasted in Firefly Amber Ale, red onions, Ohio apples and local goat cheese medallions infused with chives, black walnuts and dried cranberries.

Dressings:
Feta Cheese, Peanut Ginger, Rasoberry Wheat Vinaigrette, Balsamic, Caesar, Ranch, 1000 Island.

Firefly Roasted Chicken or Tofu | 3   Half | 1.5
```

Above is an example of Jackie O's collaborating with the local farm, Integration Acres, to source their local goat cheese for their salads.

POTENTIAL TO REACH MORE PEOPLE

Around the world, every 60 seconds, Facebook generates four million likes; Instagram users upload 48,000 photos and 300 hours of video are uploaded to YouTube. Social media sites can reach the most people with the least money. Users of social media willingly and frequently visit these sites to get updates. Sparking their interest can result in increased visibility for your cause. Also, a social media post can sometimes hold more credibility than a direct commercial advertisement.

What if my page doesn't have many "followers" or "likes"? This is a good opportunity to use your fellow producers and your current client base. Cross promotion of products in the forms of "likes" or "shares" through social media sites let your current customer base, or "fans", vouch for you to their network and/or customer base.

For example, to the right is a post from the Butcher & Grocer, a local foods store in Columbus, Ohio. The Keller Market House does a fantastic job of promoting the local dairy and brands they carry in their store by featuring them on Facebook, sometimes taking the opportunity to pair it with other brands that complement one another. By tagging Ruffwing Farms, it increases their brand visibility by however many followers the Keller Maket house has on their profile.

INCREASED BRAND AWARENESS

With regular posting and user sharing capabilities, social media can help to spread your brand and get our message out. While most consumers know what animal beef or pork comes from, they have no concept of the production process. This is the primary format be which you can tell your brand story.

COMMUNICATION WITH AN AUDIENCE

Social media can be a great way for interested people to get into contact with you to ask questions, to propose and share ideas, and to become locavore champions of your brand. You can also use it to reach out to players in your community. Social media can also be used to communicate special offerings and generate excitement over the limited quantity. To the right you can see an example of Ruffwing Farms communicating to their fans how

This Toolkit was supported by the Sustainable Agriculture Research and Education Program.

Rural Action

3

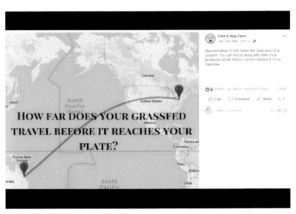

TAKE QUALITY PICTURES

A post with pictures will grab much more attention than a text post. Remember to take quality photos at events or at any point in the production process.

A blurry, pixelated, badly lit, or distracting photo will take away from the professionalism and credibility of your post. Quality imagery is important when promoting one choice over another. See the photography toolkit for more information on photography.

UTILIZE VIDEOS

One newer trend in 2018 social media is the prevalence of videos. Videos should be roughly 30-45 seconds in length and should be used to show an encounter at some point in your production process. Whether it is moving the livestock to new pasture, feeding time, how equipment or tools you use in production, or even just a short video of mixing ingredients or goats coming in from the pasture will catch the eye of your customers. You only get about two seconds of your viewers time before they will decide whether to continue watching or to scroll past.

MIX THE PERSONAL WITH THE PROMOTIONAL

Behind-the-scenes insights into your participants' businesses will add a fun and relatable tone. Pictures of piglets or calves in the field, or the sunset on the farm, offer a chance to authentically

to identify them at the Farmers Market.

LEVEL WITH COMPETITION

Big businesses and chain restaurants are using social media to promote their food. Especially when many of our participants are small business who may not have the resources to keep up with their own sites, using social media to promote local food is a great way to compete with the alternatives. You may be uncomfortable about sharing about your brand at first, but as a small business owner competing with big business, you should see yourself as a champion for your brand, ensuring that it receives the praise, awareness and customer base that it deserves.

POST REGULARLY

There is no set formula of how many times to post. People want to be engaged, but they do not like to be overwhelmed. An abandoned or underused social media site can detract from professionalism and credibility. Try to post at least once per week. Posting 1 to 3 times a day is great, but any more posts than that is not recommended.

Remember you need to keep your posts short and always attach a photo or visual to make the post more eye catching. It is recommended to keep posts under 200 words. You may find that some social media sites like Twitter and Instagram have character limits for posts.

This Toolkit was supported by the Sustainable Agriculture Research and Education Program.

connect with your consumers, many of whom may have never experienced the day to day operations required to create high quality livestock products. People are more likely to patronize a business when they feel a connection to the brand.

BE AWARE OF TIMING

Think about when people are most likely to log into social media sites. Some people check in first thing in the morning, during lunch time, towards the end of the work day, or when they get home from work. These are the best times to post as they will reach the most viewers.

VARY YOUR POSTING HABITS

Try posting on different days of the week at different times to reach members of your audience with different schedules. Sites like Facebook and Instagram offer information on post "views" or "likes" free of charge to businesses currently. Evaluate which posts have been the most successful and change your posting habits accordingly. Sites like Facebook and Instagram provide post metrics at no cost to business platforms and can help determine when you should post in order to have the greatest impression on your followers.

This Toolkit was supported by the Sustainable Agriculture Research and Education Program.

SCHEDULE POSTS IN ADVANCE

There is technology available to schedule posts hours or days before you want them to go live. Facebook has its own built in feature and there are also apps to do the same thing on other platforms, such as the app Hootsuite. If you have a busy schedule, this can help you to utilize your slowest days to your advantage. In this sample Facebook post, you see an example of scheduling the post to come out on a Saturday morning, when normally no one would be on the ACEnet social media. The blue highlighted producer names indicate that they have been "tagged" in the post and will be notified at the scheduled time.

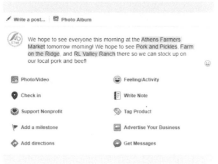

USE HASHTAGS WHEN APPROPRIATE

A hashtag is a pound sign followed by a word or phrase. It signals that a post is related to the topic identified in the hashtag. The hashtag allows social media sites to categorize posts and generate a list of all posts that have used the same hashtag.

Reliably using and promoting your brand hashtag will allow all of the social media posts that contain it to be organized into one feed when the hashtag is clicked on. You can also use other food related hashtags to try to gain visibility from people surfing through popular hashtags. Some popular hashtags for the local food movement include: #localfood #locavore #slowfood #ecofoodie #foodie #profood.

5

Check your local area and events to find out if there is a local hashtag that you can incorporate to reach local audiences. A quick social media search can let you know how many times the hashtag has been used and what others are using it for.

TAG AND INTERACT WITH CUSTOMERS AND SUPPORTERS

Your local specialty dairy brand has a great support system. Even a start-up operation has fans and loyal customers. Tagging retail stores, restaurant customers, Farmers Markets, and encouraging customers to "tag" you in return will help with two things. First, it will increase the likelihood that more people will see your post. Some users might be following an organization, project or business that you tagged in a post, and they will indirectly view your post as a result, which increases the chances that they will click on your page, see your other posts, and get involved.

Second, it will increase the responses that you get on your posts. When you tag participants and partners, you are appealing to people who you already know who care about local meat, local farms and the local food economy. They will hopefully like or comment on your post. On some social media sites, posts with the most interaction are shown first to users scrolling though the feed.

INTERACT WITH YOUR AUDIENCE

Frame your posts so that they invite interaction from your followers. Ask them questions or invite them to participate in concrete ways. Respond to comments in a positive way and respond to messages in a timely manner. Follow people or projects in your community and pay attention when they post about your meat products, your farm or your retail business.

Remember that on social media your business will be in the same space as your customers' friends. Your posts are competing with those personal networks. Instead of only promoting your business, use your page to build a community. People genuinely enjoy learning about hte day to day stories and interests of your business rather than advertising. Neighborly approaches make businesses more familiar to potential customers and create positive feelings about your brand.

This Toolkit was supported by the Sustainable Agriculture Research and Education Program.

6

XVII. ACENET DESIGNING YOUR BRAND IDENTITY: PHOTOGRAPHY

BUILDING A BRAND FOR SPECIALTY DAIRY

DESIGNING YOUR BRAND IDENTITY: *PHOTOGRAPHY*

November 7, 2018

OUR HELPFUL TECHNIQUES AND CONSIDERATIONS

Taking great photographs requires a certain frame of mind. There are many factors that go into a good picture, but the camera takes only a split second to snap the picture, and it's hard to focus on everything at once during that moment.

While trained professionals will always take the best photos, there are things you can do to take great photos for your brand on your budget. Keeping your goals in mind can help you to snap the right shots. Thinking about photographic elements can help take your photography to the next level.

KEEPING YOUR BRAND'S PHOTOGRAPHIC STYLE

Keeping your brand's photographic style in mind will help to keep your photos on track!
Your imagery should revolve around your products. Capture not only the garnished final products, but all stages in the process. Photograph the sources of ingredients and nutrients, the processes of food creation, creative chefs at work, and wise farmers perfecting their craft.

Portray the lifestyle that comes with local food. Convey a strong sense of unique place and atmosphere. Capture what is unique about your community and each dish. Capture different dining atmospheres. Portray hard work, business development, and success along the way. Look for genuine smiles!

Use a quality image capturing device. The first step to professional looking photos is having the right tools. Use the best device that is accessible to you. Auto-focusing cameras don't always correctly guess what you are taking a picture of. Make sure that the important part of the photo is the part in focus. Stand still to take photos. Make sure your lens is not foggy.
Don't distort images by disproportionately stretching, squashing, or skewing them.

FRAMING

Consider the entire frame of your photographs. Primarily, your focus will be on your subject, but the rest of the frame is just as important. Review the following:

• What is in the foreground (in front of your subject?)
• What is in the background?
• Does anything in the photo make the scene feel unprofessional or interfere with the mood you want to convey?
• Do you need to rearrange or alter the scene to

This Toolkit was supported by the Sustainable Agriculture Research and Education Program.

7

control what is in the frame?
• Is anything being cut off?
• What else could be included in the frame if you zoomed out?
• What could be really focused on if you zoomed in?
• How does the photo change if you frame it vertically as opposed to horizontally?

The frame created by your camera might not be the shape that you want in the end. What will you use this photo for? What sort of shape will you need to crop it to?

VANTAGE POINT

Consider different vantage points from which to take each photo. Most people will take pictures of what they see at eye level without thinking about other views. Sometimes those pictures turn out great, but a more interesting, unique angle can be more compelling than an unconsidered, common vantage point.

What is the typical vantage point from which your subject is most often seen? What would happen if you took the photo from below? What would the photo look like from a bird's eye view? What other angles might work?

Consider all 360 degrees around your subject. If you stood somewhere else, would the background be better? Would the overall photo be better?

LIGHTING

Light makes photography possible. Some lighting conditions are better than others. The ideal light for photography is soft, indirect, natural sunlight. Harsh bright light can cause squinting and make subjects look unnatural or blown out.

Only use the flash on your camera as a last resort, when the scene cannot be brightened any other way.

Photos tend to be especially discolored when different kinds of light sources are mixed together,

such as natural sunlight and artificial light bulbs. Indoor artificial lighting can cause your photos to look discolored by throwing off the white balance, or the designation of what is "white," in your photo. Try to limit your light source to one kind of light to get the truest colors. To limit artificial light, turn them off, shoot near a window, or go outside. Ways to limit sunlight include shooting indoors at night and avoiding windows. You can also combat discoloration from lighting by adjusting the white balance on your camera, if that is an option for you. Consider lighting when you decide on a vantage point. If your light source is behind your subject, your subject will look dark. If the only light source is pointed directly at your subject, your subject may look too light or too flat. It's best to have light hitting your subject at an indirect angle.

Can you tell the difference in the pasta sauce pictures below? The one on far left was taken in a controlled setting, with a digital camera. The one in the middle was taken in mixed lighting and on the far right the picture was taken outside with the light from behind.

PHOTOGRAPHY'S PURPOSE

Your brand's purpose is to show local food in a great light, and photography is one of the best ways to

This Toolkit was supported by the Sustainable Agriculture Research and Education Program.

8

do that. Whether you're photographing a plated dish, a raw ingredient, or packaged products, these techniques can help.

Try photographing the process that creates the food, whether that be farming, cooking, packaging, or something else. You can also try photographing the finished product next to the ingredients, seeds, or tools that it was created with.

Think about what is the most appealing about this food and emphasize that trait:

• Is it the texture?
• The presentation?
• The overall scene?
• The color?
• A certain ingredient?

You can't be afraid to move the product around. Set a scene. Work on presentation. Use props! Think about colors and textures that will really make this food shine. Consider items like plates, cutlery, tables, tablecloths, baskets, cooking utensils, shopping carts, and etcetera. Make sure your props are cleanand flattering. Make sure the food looks appetizing. Consider adding garnishes, or drizzling sauces.

Let a retailer know in advance that you intend to photograph dairy products in their store for promotion. They might have ideas or props to improve the presentation. Try photographing someone interacting with the food in a natural way.

PHOTOGRAPHY ETHICS

Stock photos and photos taken from the Internet will never be truly genuine, but when we need to use them, we need to be ethical. We need to make sure that there are not copyright restrictions on them. Photographers and artists work hard to produce photos and clip-art! You will need to search for photos that specifically do not have copyright protections, because by default all images are copyrighted to their photographers. You will need to search for photos in the public domain or photos protected under a Creative Commons license. An Internet search will help you find sites with photo archives in the public domain or protected by a Creative Commons license.

PUBLIC DOMAIN & CREATIVE COMMONS

Photos in the public domain do not have any copyright protections, for whatever reason. Photos with a Creative Commons license will allow free use under specific guidelines. You will need to read those guidelines to find out if the photographer wants you to cite him or her as a source and if you are allowed to use it in your situation.

This Toolkit was supported by the Sustainable Agriculture Research and Education Program.

9

XVIII. LOYALTY CARD EXAMPLE

Lucky Penny Farm

XIX. SPECIAL EVENT TEMPLATE

Budget Sample (Based on number of attendees
*Adapted from UCLA Budget

Name of Event
Day of week, Date(s) and Time
Location

Audio/Visual and Technical
   Sound system- microphone, iPod connection, set-up, delivery
   Projection equipment- 2 screens, 2 projectors, splitter connection

Catering and Beverage
   Tray-pass hors d'oeuvres – 5 pieces each @ $0/person
   Dinner – including 3-courses @ $0/person
   Bar service – Hosted @ $0/person including glassware, staffing and service
      through reception and dinner
   Staffing, service charge and tax for meals
   Catering cost per person (# people)
   Staff/musician meals – 15 @ $0/person

Design and Décor
   Registration table florals – 2 @ $0/each
   Centerpieces – 10@ $0/each
   Floral delivery and tax
   Stage décor, including delivery and tax

Entertainment
   Music/band
   Stage

Facilities
   Grounds – dumpsters/porta-potty rental
   Custodial services – pre and post event, including site cleanup

Parking/Transportation
  Attendants - 2@ $0/hour
  Signage – parking/pedestrian signs, 10@ $0/each
  Courtesy parking for VIP guests – # cars @ $0/each
  Space posting fee/barricades
  Traffic enforcement officer – 2 @ $0/hour
  Parking shuttle

Photography/Videography
  Photographer
  Videographer

Postage/Mail Processing
  Mail housing processing – stuffing, stamping, labeling, mailing

Program
  Speaker fee
  Airfare and transportation – 1 economy-class ticket and taxi
  Hotel for speaker – 1 night @ $0/night, including tax
  Meals for speaker, exclusive of event catering

Promotional Materials/Collateral
  Design fee
  Printing fee

Publicity/Marketing
  Paid advertising – traditional/nontraditional

Rentals
  Registration – 6' tables, chairs and linens, coat rack
  Cocktail areas – stand up and sit down tables, chairs, linens, heaters, glassware
  Guest seating – 66" rounds, chiavari chairs, premium linens, table service, glassware
  Kitchen – 30' tent, kitchen equipment
  Other – easels, trellis, generator
  On-site staff
  Tax, delivery and staffing

Security/Safety
   Police – 2 plain-clothes officers @ $0/hour for 2 hours
   Wheelchair rental, 1 @ $0/each

Signage (Event Signage)
   General event signage – 5@ $0/each
   Parking signage

Supplies and Miscellaneous
   Name tags, table number supplies, registration supplies, miscellaneous supplies

Other Stuff You Forgot

Miscellaneous Contingency – 10%

TOTAL

Reviewed by Staff Members   Initial   Date
_____

_____

Please have all associated staff read and initial

XIX. SPECIAL EVENT TEMPLATE

Continued...
Event Fact Sheet
*Adapted from UCLA Event Fact Sheet

Name of Event
Day of week, Date(s) and Time
Location

Purpose: Goals and objectives of the event; statement of purpose

Background: Background information on the event, honored participants, important history or details

Guests: Guest category list (speakers, customers, volunteers, community, private party). Number of guests

Format: - Event: List basic event format and series of events/activities
  - Is there a theme? Special requests?
  - Program Order: Actual start time
  - List program participants and their role

Budget: Approved budget and event manager name for approvals
  day of the event

Statistics: - Invitations: Total number of invitations sent/how
  - Accepted: Number of acceptances/RSVPs
  (eventbright/brown paper tickets)
  - Actual: Actual number of attendees
  - Walk-ons: Number of walk-on guests
  - Cost/person: Final budget divided by number of actual
  attendees

Partner(s): List of partnering organizations/individuals

Contact: Name of event manager, phone and email

XIX. SPECIAL EVENT TEMPLATE

Continued...
Event-Planning Strategic Questions
*Adapted from UCLA Event-Planning Strategic Questions

Events are critical tools for building your brand. Review the questions below and share with your team to ensure a successful event experience.

Goals and Objectives
- What are the key goals and objectives of this event?
- What is the desired outcome and what do you want your guests to take away from this experience?
- Is an event the best or most appropriate way to achieve your goals (versus, for example, a press release or other targeted communication, social media, etc.)?
- What is the long-term value of the activity of your business?
- How will you gauge the effectiveness of your event? (client/audience survey, media coverage)

Communications and Marketing
What is your event's primary message and theme?
- If you will have speakers, who would be appropriate?
- If there are multiple speakers, how would their messages be appropriately differentiated and integrated?
- How will this program be choreographed?
- What other elements may be incorporated to convey the message? (i.e. video, music, visuals, tours, food)

What are the ways this event will be marketed?
- How can we gain greater effectiveness/leverage from this event – before and after?
- Hire a photographer to capture experiences

How will your message be communicated or reinforced?
- Promotional materials (save the date, invite, program)
- Event calendar (happenings)
- Website
- Social media (Facebook, Twitter, Instagram, etc.)
- Publications (newsletters)
- Advertising
- Media story
- Local/national media

Do the promotional materials (design and copy) clearly reflect/identify your business/logo, contact information?

Planning and Production

Who is paying for the event and what is the budgeted amount?

Who is the target audience?
- What mechanism/groups/mailing list will you use to reach them?
- Who else might benefit from this event beyond the primary attendees?

Are there opportunities to partner/collaborate with other farms?

What is the best date and location for this event?
- Time of year
- Location (size, type/style of venue, parking)
- Will the time or location of this event be affected by other events happening at/around the same time? (Earth Day, college football, Mother's Day, other holidays)